PASSING THE NORTH CAROLINA THIRD GRADE EOG TEST IN MATHEMATICS

THE COMPETITIVE EDGE

R. HOMER ANDREWS
ELEMENTARY SCHOOL

JANE HEREFORD

CPC — *CONTEMPORARY PUBLISHING COMPANY OF RALEIGH, INC.*
6001-101 Chapel Hill Road, Raleigh, NC 27607 • (919) 851-8221

Publisher: Charles E. Grantham
Marketing Director: Sherri Powell
Production Manager: Erika J. Mason
Cover Design: Pam Varney / Piedmont Lithographers
Typesetting: Contemporary Publishing Company of Raleigh, Inc.
Printer: Edwards Brothers, Inc.

ISBN: 0-89892-186-4

Copyright © 1999, Contemporary Publishing Company of Raleigh, Inc.

All rights reserved. No part of this publication may be reproduced, stored in a retrieval system, or transmitted, in any form or by any means, electronic, mechanical, photocopying, recording, or otherwise, without the prior written permission of the publisher.

Printed in the United States of America

10   9   8   7   6   5   4   3   2

TABLE OF CONTENTS

1	Whole Numbers	1
2	Money	29
3	Fractions	45
4	Estimating	66
5	Number Lines	72
6	Measurements	76
7	Geometry	98
8	Area	113
9	Perimeter	120
10	Volume	126
11	Coordinate Planes, Translations, Reflections, and Rotations	139
12	Tables, Graphs, Maps, Thermometers, and Calendars	151
13	Number Patterns	166

Practice Test 1

Practice Test 2

To the Student

The 3rd Grade EOG in math is a very important test that you should take seriously.

Some of you will be asked to attend summer school this summer if you fail this test. Others of you may repeat the 3rd grade if you fail this test. Therefore, it is necessary for you to learn all the concepts in this book.

"I hope that you will learn to work all the problems correctly. Study, concentrate, and work hard. Good luck on your 3rd grade EOG in math!!!"

To the Teacher

Most schools have had a hard time finding the "perfect" book for teaching the math for the 3rd grade EOG. There isn't one!! So, I decided to write this book to help the teachers who are teaching math in the 3rd grade.

No, this book is not "perfect," but I have tried to put in an adequate number of problems for the average 3rd grade student. Most students will grasp the concepts after working through the chapters, others will not. You will have to supplement with other resources for these students.

"I have enjoyed putting this book together because it meets a great need. Good luck in helping your math students achieve their goal — passing the 3rd grade EOG in math!!"

WHOLE NUMBERS

CHAPTER 1

PLACE VALUE

6 thousands 1 hundreds 2 tens 4 ones

PRACTICE

Name the place value of each underlined number.

1. 5,00<u>0</u> _____
2. 5,<u>1</u>25 _____
3. 2,<u>4</u>51 _____
4. 3,7<u>0</u>2 _____
5. <u>3</u>,211 _____
6. <u>6</u>,750 _____
7. <u>8</u>62 _____
8. 3,6<u>0</u>7 _____
9. 3,<u>4</u>07 _____
10. 1,8<u>5</u>6 _____

11. <u>7</u>56 _____
12. 2,01<u>6</u> _____
13. <u>1</u>,376 _____
14. 3,88<u>2</u> _____
15. 3<u>6</u> _____
16. 4,<u>8</u>00 _____
17. 1,<u>3</u>64 _____
18. 4,17<u>8</u> _____
19. 13<u>7</u> _____
20. <u>9</u>,761 _____

WRITING NUMBERS

EXAMPLES

<u>5,129</u>

1. To write this number in words, underline the numbers separated by commas.
2. Write the numbers in words (from left to right)) that you underlined leaving a space for the comma.

- five_____one hundred twenty-nine

3. Fill in the space with the word for the comma. (Commas are named from right to left.) First comma = thousand.

five thousand, one hundred twenty-nine

(two) <u>thousand</u> (five hundred nineteen)

1. To write this number in standard form, first, underline the word that represents the comma (thousand).
2. Put parentheses around the words that represent numbers.
3. Write the numbers that represent the words and put a comma in the place of the underlined word.

- 2,519

PRACTICE

Write each number in words.

1. 9,243 _____

2. 1,200 _____

3. 5,124 _____

4. 9,941 _____

5. 8,310 _____

6. 4,100 _____

7. 220 _____

8. 4,402 _____

9. 2,007 _____

10. 487 _____

11. 100 _____

12. 6,017 _____

13. 9,999 _____

14. 5,143 _____

15. 366 _____

Write each in standard form.

16. two thousand, eighteen

_____

17. one thousand, eighty-four

_____

18. nine thousand, seventy-five

_____

19. three thousand, four hundred twenty-one

_____

20. three thousand, seventy-one

_____

21. one hundred, twenty-two

_____

(continued on next page)

22. nine thousand, nine hundred
_____

23. five thousand, eleven
_____

24. two thousand, one hundred one
_____

25. seven hundred ninety-one
_____

26. two thousand, four hundred twenty-three
_____

27. six thousand, nine hundred
_____

28. one hundred seventy-two
_____

29. seven thousand, nine hundred fifty-eight
_____

30. nine thousand, seven
_____

EXPANDED FORM

To write numbers in expanded form, write the numbers as an addition problem of place values.

EXAMPLES

5,124 ➡ 5,000 + 100 + 20 + 4

361 ➡ 300 + 60 + 1

PRACTICE

Write each number in expanded form.

1. 4,653 _____
2. 136 _____
3. 4,213 _____
4. 568 _____
5. 321 _____
6. 2,502 _____
7. 7,002 _____
8. 367 _____
9. 3,867 _____
10. 93 _____
11. 5,113 _____
12. 9,786 _____
13. 9,379 _____
14. 83 _____
15. 3,101 _____
16. 9,204 _____
17. 1,399 _____
18. 9,924 _____
19. 1,003 _____
20. 436 _____

Copyright © 1999 Contemporary Publishing Company of Raleigh, Inc.

OTHER WAYS TO WRITE NUMBERS

EXAMPLES

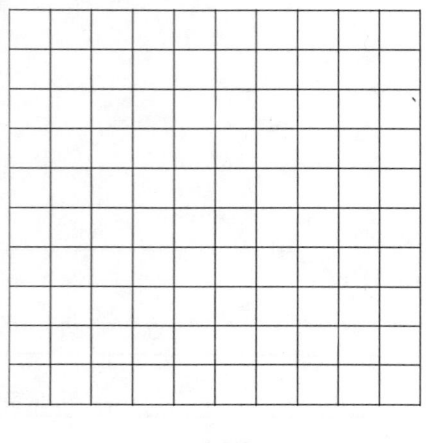

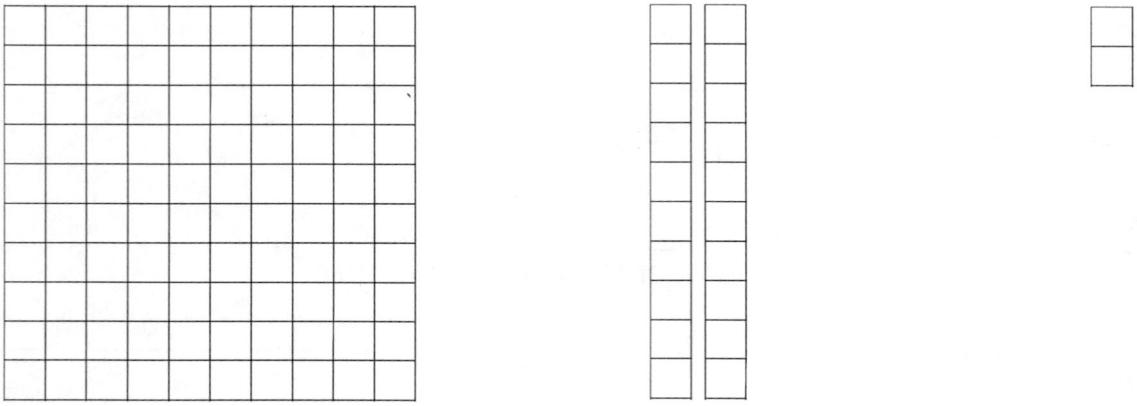

100   +   20   +   2   = 122

◯ = 100   △ = 10   ☐ = 1

◯◯◯   △△   ☐☐   = 322

PRACTICE

Write each in standard form.

1. 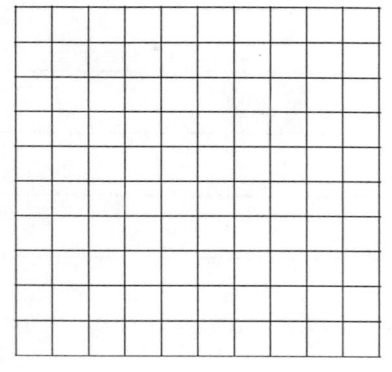   _____

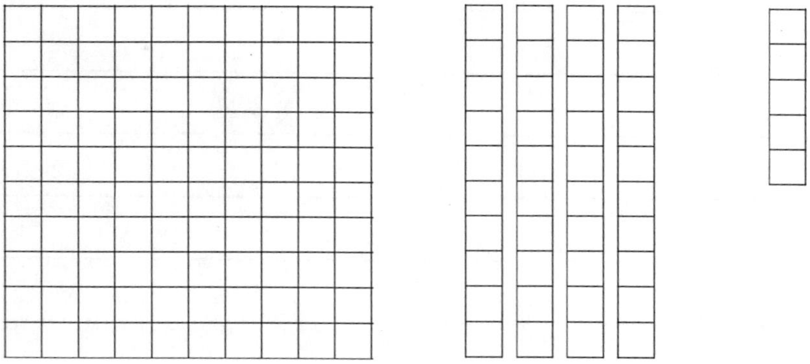

2. 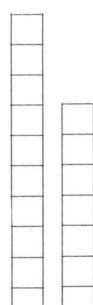 _____

3. 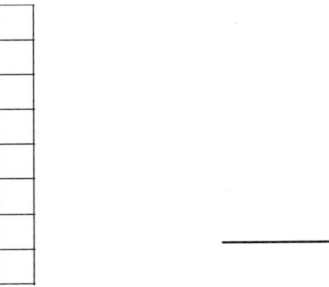 _____

4. 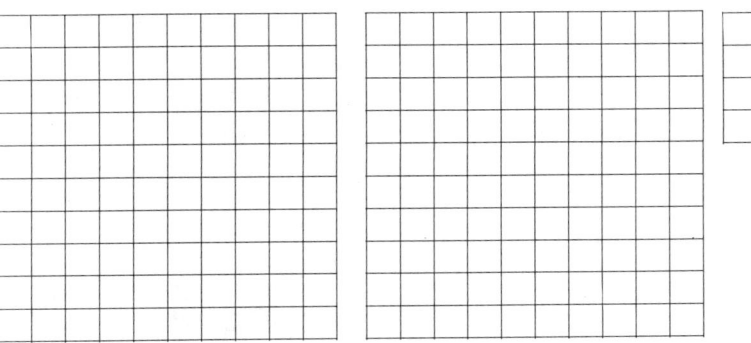 _____

5. 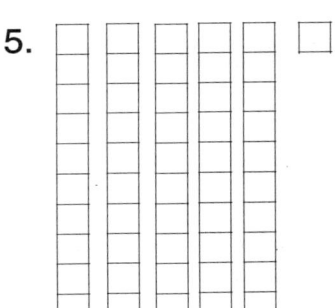 _____

Use the following for # 6 – 10.   ◯ = 100   △ = 10   ☐ = 1

6. ◯◯◯◯ △ ☐☐☐ _____

7. △△△△△△△ ☐ _____

8. ◯ ☐☐☐ _____

9. ◯◯◯◯◯◯ △ ☐☐☐☐☐ _____

10. ☐☐☐☐☐☐☐☐ _____

7

ORDERING NUMBERS

Numbers are ordered by the way you count. 1, 2, 3, 4, 5, 6, 7, 8, 9, etc. Following this order, 1 is less than 2, 2 is less than 3, and so on. Still following the order, 2 is greater than 1, 3 is greater than 2, and so on.

EXAMPLES

10, 5, 11, 3, 2, 1, 7

List these numbers in order from smallest to largest.

1, 2, 3, 5, 7, 10, 11

List these same numbers from smallest to largest.

11, 10, 7, 2, 3, 2, 1

PRACTICE

Write the numbers in order from smallest to largest.

1. 25, 40, 39, 21, 14, 3, 7 _____

2. 93, 75, 100, 5, 15, 14, 30 _____

3. 236, 512, 721, 174, 207, 819 _____

4. 57, 80, 149, 24, 111, 200, 717 _____

5. 300, 412, 201, 49, 374, 122 _____

6. 999, 143, 700, 221, 566, 49 _____

7. 20, 40, 10, 5, 18, 36, 81, 11 _____

8. 621, 700, 827, 911, 321, 632, 707 _____

9. 92, 94, 86, 89, 27, 21, 35, 40 _____

10. 1,200, 2,401, 1,345, 1,217, 1,350 _____

List the following numbers in order from largest to smallest.

11. 8, 6, 14, 29, 32, 1, 12, 16 _____

12. 87, 92, 67, 55, 101, 29, 217, 56 _____

13. 1,111, 2,406, 3,846, 1,247, 1,493, 762

_____

14. 126, 245, 100, 79, 386, 143, 27 _____

15. 367, 361, 368, 360, 362, 366, 369_____

16. 9,129, 9,245, 9,117, 9,200, 9,145, 9,133

_____

17. 29, 39, 19, 27, 17, 37, 40, 47, 49 _____

18. 3, 19, 2, 86, 15, 21, 13, 20 _____

19. 751, 601, 753, 750, 600, 519, 500_____

20. 120, 1,230, 119, 246, 1,717, 300 _____

EVEN AND ODD NUMBERS

Even Numbers   2, 4, 6, 8, 10, 12, 14, 16 . . .

Odd Numbers   1, 3, 5, 7, 9, 11, 13, 15 . . .

EXAMPLES

What is the next even number after 12? $12^{+2} = 14$

What is the next odd number after 15? $15^{+2} = 17$

PRACTICE

Write whether each number is even or odd.

1. 100 _____   11. 240 _____

2. 220 _____   12. 862 _____

3. 117 _____   13. 210 _____

4. 80 _____   14. 79 _____

5. 93 _____   15. 41 _____

6. 76 _____   16. 36 _____

7. 92 _____   17. 945 _____

8. 110 _____   18. 1,000 _____

9. 33 _____   19. 9 _____

10. 17 _____   20. 37 _____

ROUNDING

EXAMPLES

Round to the nearest hundred.
1|63 = 200

number to stay the same or go up 1

Round to the nearest ten.
7|1

number to stay the same or go up 1

The one is in the hundreds place, so look at the number to the right of 1. (0–4 stays the same. 5–9 goes up one.)

Six is the number to the right, so the 1 will go up to 2. Numbers behind the line change to zeroes. 163 rounds to 200.

The 7 is in the tens place with 1 to the right. 1 will keep the 7 the same. Numbers behind the line change to zeroes. 71 rounds to 70.

ADDING

EXAMPLES

```
  6 ⎫    6
  7 ⎬   +7
       ―――
         13
 +5      +5
 ――     ―――
 18      18
```

```
   436
 + 542
 ―――――
   978
```

Add each row from right to left.

```
  1 1 1
  6,875
+ 1,345
―――――――
  8,220
```

From right to left, add each row. Carry extra digit to the next row.

Copyright © 1999 Contemporary Publishing Company of Raleigh, Inc.

PRACTICE

Add.

1. 4 + 3 + 1

2. 8 + 8 + 6

3. 46 + 23

4. 6,237 + 8,799

5. 644 + 305 + 137

6. 6,423 + 1,484 + 526

7. 7 + 11 + 7

8. 10 + 10 + 15 + 6

9. 127 + 843

10. 2,914 + 4,023

11. 1,348 + 2,974

12. 6,957 + 488 + 8,291

13. 5,938 + 6,375 + 983

14. 7,468 + 874 + 7,647

15. 1,865 + 7,700 + 835

16. 9,278 + 3,947

17. 7,488 + 5,869 + 23

18. 417 + 58 + 9 + 100

SUBTRACTING

No Borrowing

EXAMPLES

```
   7        18        734
 - 3       - 3       - 120
   4        15        614
```

Subtract each row from right to left.

PRACTICE

Subtract.

1. 62 − 21

2. 849 − 434

3. 9,089 − 5,038

4. 8,836 − 3,623

5. 7,658 − 2,427

6. 39 − 27

7. 503 − 81

8. 483 − 202

9. 287 − 87

10. 69 − 12

(continued on next page)

11. 487 − 313

12. 8,572 − 1,151

13. 4,271 − 2,150

14. 4,704 − 2,201

15. 3,486 − 2,100

16. 5,624 − 4,213

17. 8,964 − 5,821

18. 8,895 − 7,802

19. 5,128 − 2,127

20. 3,400 − 1,200

21. 862 − 32

22. 9,123 − 110

23. 8,145 − 8,132

24. 8,999 − 7,364

SUBTRACTING
BORROWING

EXAMPLES

$$\begin{array}{r} 4\overset{8}{\cancel{9}}\overset{13}{\cancel{3}} \\ -214 \\ \hline 279 \end{array}$$

You cannot subtract 4 from 3. You must borrow a 10 from the 90. 3 becomes 13. 9 becomes 8. Now subtract from right to left.

$$\begin{array}{r} \overset{3}{\cancel{4}}\overset{10}{\cancel{1}}\overset{12}{\cancel{3}}\overset{10}{\cancel{0}} \\ -1987 \\ \hline 2143 \end{array}$$

In this problem, you must borrow many times. Start from right to left.

PRACTICE

Subtract.

1. 482 – 175

2. 459 – 160

3. 1,653 – 181

4. 8,463 – 2,171

5. 696 – 359

6. 3,278 – 1,589

7. 7,593 – 3,897

8. 363 – 215

(continued on next page)

9. 374 − 282

10. 5,157 − 589

11. 729 − 268

12. 918 − 484

13. 526 − 187

14. 6,613 − 355

15. 7,436 − 749

16. 8,313 − 438

17. 7,700 − 3,718

18. 4,000 − 281

19. 6,142 − 3,264

20. 4,103 − 1,315

21. 9,000 − 7,341

22. 1,123 − 873

23. 4,001 − 3,456

24. 8,075 − 249

REVIEW

1. What is the place value of the 5 in 2,513?
   a. tens
   b. hundreds
   c. ones

2. What number do you get when you round 4,587 to the nearest ten?
   a. 4,600
   b. 5,000
   c. 4,580
   d. 4,590

3. There were 3,726 women and 5,277 men in the gym. How many people were in the gym?
   a. 251
   b. 9,003
   c. 4,876
   d. 8,103

4. To the nearest thousand, how many fish are in the pond?

Fish	Number in pond
Catfish	2,145
Bass	365
Pike	4,220
Trout	1,936

   a. 7,000
   b. 6,000
   c. 9,000
   d. 8,000

5. Sharon bought a ten... sleeping bag for $60, ... $80. Which of the foll... determine how much S... spent?
   a. $700 − $60 + $80
   b. $700 − $60 − $80
   c. $700 + $60 − $80
   d. $700 + $60 + $80

6. Gary paid for $85 worth of groceries with $90. How much change did he receive?
   a. $15
   b. $5
   c. $135
   d. $0

7. Round 145 to the nearest hundred.
   a. 200
   b. 140
   c. 100
   d. 150

8. What is the total cost of a boat selling for $5,886 and a motor for $1,059?
   a. $5,027
   b. $7,945
   c. $5,945
   d. $6,945

What is the sum of $500, $800, $8,000, and $600?
a. $9,900
b. $9,800
c. $8,800
d. $8,900

10. 6,000 + 300 + 13 in standard form is _____.
a. 3,136
b. 3,631
c. 6,013
d. 6,313

11. Round 302 to the nearest hundred.
a. 200
b. 310
c. 400
d. 300

12. Clarence paid $6,838 for a used car. Marilyn paid $3,220 less than Clarence. How much did Marilyn pay for her car?
a. $8,258
b. $3,610
c. $3,618
d. $8,268

13. Round 975 to the nearest hundred.
a. 900
b. 980
c. 1,000
d. 990

14. The balance on a credit card account is $1,175. Karen paid $250. To find the new balance, which of the following would you use?
a. $1,175 − $250
b. $1,175 + $250
c. $250 − $1,175
d. $250 + $1,175

15. The attendance at a football game was 8,126. Last week's game had 350 more people. What was last week's attendance?
a. 7,776
b. 8,563
c. 8,476
d. 7,876

16. Which of the following is 3,463 in expanded form?
a. 3,000 + 463
b. 3,000 + 400 + 60 + 3
c. 3 + 46 + 3
d. 3 + 400 + 60 + 3

17. What is the total cost of groceries ($36.50), clothes ($167.25), and medicine ($56.75)?
a. $250.00
b. $260.50
c. $360.50
d. $350.00

18. To the nearest ten, which number is the largest?

   (2,455) (2,454)
   (2,425) (2,443)

   a. 2,454
   b. 2,443
   c. 2,425
   d. 2,455

19. 8,925 is which of the following in words?
   a. eight nine two five
   b. eight hundred ninety twenty-five
   c. eight thousand, nine hundred twenty-five
   d. eight thousand, nine twenty-five

20. What is one thousand, two hundred thirty in standard form?
   a. 1,000, 230
   b. 1,230
   c. 230
   d. 123

21. 2,000 + 200 + 10 + 7 is what in standard form?
   a. 2,107
   b. 2,217
   c. 217
   d. 107

22.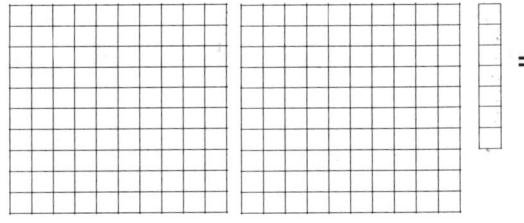

   a. 277
   b. 27
   c. 270
   d. 207

23. { = 100 | = 10 ↑ = 1
   so {{{ | | | | ↑↑ =
   a. 342
   b. 234
   c. 432
   d. 3,402

24.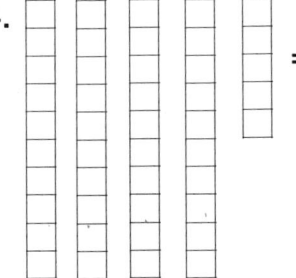

   a. 50
   b. 45
   c. 405
   d. 445

MULTIPLICATION FACTS

1

1 × 0 = 0
1 × 1 = 1
1 × 2 = 2
1 × 3 = 3
1 × 4 = 4
1 × 5 = 5
1 × 6 = 6
1 × 7 = 7
1 × 8 = 8
1 × 9 = 9
1 × 10 = 10
1 × 11 = 11
1 × 12 = 12

2

2 × 0 = 0
2 × 1 = 2
2 × 2 = 4
2 × 3 = 6
2 × 4 = 8
2 × 5 = 10
2 × 6 = 12
2 × 7 = 14
2 × 8 = 16
2 × 9 = 18
2 × 10 = 20
2 × 11 = 22
2 × 12 = 24

3

3 × 0 = 0
3 × 1 = 3
3 × 2 = 6
3 × 3 = 9
3 × 4 = 12
3 × 5 = 15
3 × 6 = 18
3 × 7 = 21
3 × 8 = 24
3 × 9 = 27
3 × 10 = 30
3 × 11 = 33
3 × 12 = 36

4

4 × 0 = 0
4 × 1 = 4
4 × 2 = 8
4 × 3 = 12
4 × 4 = 16
4 × 5 = 20
4 × 6 = 24
4 × 7 = 28
4 × 8 = 32
4 × 9 = 36
4 × 10 = 40
4 × 11 = 44
4 × 12 = 48

5

5 × 0 = 0
5 × 1 = 5
5 × 2 = 10
5 × 3 = 15
5 × 4 = 20
5 × 5 = 25
5 × 6 = 30
5 × 7 = 35
5 × 8 = 40
5 × 9 = 45
5 × 10 = 50
5 × 11 = 55
5 × 12 = 60

6

6 × 0 = 0
6 × 1 = 6
6 × 2 = 12
6 × 3 = 18
6 × 4 = 24
6 × 5 = 30
6 × 6 = 36
6 × 7 = 42
6 × 8 = 48
6 × 9 = 54
6 × 10 = 60
6 × 11 = 66
6 × 12 = 72

Copyright © 1999 Contemporary Publishing Company of Raleigh, Inc.

MULTIPLICATION FACTS

7

7 × 0 = 0
7 × 1 = 7
7 × 2 = 14
7 × 3 = 21
7 × 4 = 28
7 × 5 = 35
7 × 6 = 42
7 × 7 = 49
7 × 8 = 56
7 × 9 = 63
7 × 10 = 70
7 × 11 = 77
7 × 12 = 84

8

8 × 0 = 0
8 × 1 = 8
8 × 2 = 16
8 × 3 = 24
8 × 4 = 32
8 × 5 = 40
8 × 6 = 48
8 × 7 = 56
8 × 8 = 64
8 × 9 = 72
8 × 10 = 80
8 × 11 = 88
8 × 12 = 96

9

9 × 0 = 0
9 × 1 = 9
9 × 2 = 18
9 × 3 = 27
9 × 4 = 36
9 × 5 = 45
9 × 6 = 54
9 × 7 = 63
9 × 8 = 72
9 × 9 = 81
9 × 10 = 90
9 × 11 = 99
9 × 12 = 108

10

10 × 0 = 0
10 × 1 = 10
10 × 2 = 20
10 × 3 = 30
10 × 4 = 40
10 × 5 = 50
10 × 6 = 60
10 × 7 = 70
10 × 8 = 80
10 × 9 = 90
10 × 10 = 100
10 × 11 = 110
10 × 12 = 120

11

11 × 0 = 0
11 × 1 = 11
11 × 2 = 22
11 × 3 = 33
11 × 4 = 44
11 × 5 = 55
11 × 6 = 66
11 × 7 = 77
11 × 8 = 88
11 × 9 = 99
11 × 10 = 110
11 × 11 = 121
11 × 12 = 132

12

12 × 0 = 0
12 × 1 = 12
12 × 2 = 24
12 × 3 = 36
12 × 4 = 48
12 × 5 = 60
12 × 6 = 72
12 × 7 = 84
12 × 8 = 96
12 × 9 = 108
12 × 10 = 120
12 × 11 = 132
12 × 12 = 144

Copyright © 1999 Contemporary Publishing Company of Raleigh, Inc.

PRACTICE

Answer the following by using the multiplication facts.

1. 5 × □ = 25

2. □ × 9 = 54

3. 4 × □ = 36

4. □ × 2 = 10

5. 12 × □ = 24

6. □ × 5 = 40

7. 11 × □ = 33

8. □ × 3 = 24

9. 7 × □ = 28

10. □ × 10 = 50

11. 5 × □ = 45

12. □ × 8 = 64

13. 6 × □ = 42

14. □ × 9 = 72

15. 6 × □ = 36

16. 8 × 7 = □

17. 9 × 3 = □

18. 4 × 4 = □

19. 12 × 12 = □

20. 10 × 11 = □

21. 2 × 0 = □

22. 5 × 7 = □

23. 4 × 8 = □

24. 2 × 12 = □

25. 3 × 9 = □

26. 7 × 9 = □

27. 3 × 1 = □

28. 4 × 2 = □

29. 10 × 10 = □

30. 7 × 7 = □

DIVISION FACTS

EXAMPLES

$\square \div 6 = 2$ Think: $6 \times 2 = 12$ $27 \div \square = 9$ Think: $9 \times 3 = 27$
              $12 \div 6 = 2$ $27 \div 3 = 9$

PRACTICE

Divide.

1. $\square \div 3 = 9$

2. $\square \div 2 = 8$

3. $\square \div 10 = 4$

4. $\square \div 4 = 9$

5. $\square \div 6 = 8$

6. $\square \div 7 = 8$

7. $\square \div 8 = 9$

8. $32 \div \square = 8$

9. $45 \div \square = 5$

10. $100 \div \square = 10$

11. $56 \div \square = 7$

12. $35 \div \square = 7$

13. $64 \div \square = 8$

14. $54 \div 6 = \square$

15. $81 \div 9 = \square$

16. $40 \div 5 = \square$

17. $9 \div 3 = \square$

18. $18 \div 3 = \square$

19. $27 \div 3 = \square$

20. $24 \div \square = 6$

21. $16 \div \square = 4$

22. $24 \div \square = 8$

23. $\square \div 2 = 11$

24. $\square \div 7 = 7$

25. $\square \div 9 = 7$

DIVISION

MODELING DIVISION

9 ÷ 3 or 3)9

○ ○ ○ ○ ○ ○ ○ ○ ○

1. The 9 is how many units (circles) are needed.

[○ ○ ○][○ ○ ○][○ ○ ○]

2. The 3 is how many units are in each group.
3. There are 3 groups of 3 in 9. Therefore, 9 ÷ 3 is 3.

EXAMPLES

Draw a model for 12 ÷ 6.

[○ ○ ○ ○ ○ ○][○ ○ ○ ○ ○ ○]

12 ÷ 6 = 2

PRACTICE

Draw a model for each division problem. Solve to find quotient.

1. 10 ÷ 2

2. 15 ÷ 5

3. 8 ÷ 4

4. 18 ÷ 6

5. 15 ÷ 3

6. 10 ÷ 5

7. 14 ÷ 7

8. 12 ÷ 3

REVIEW

1. Which of the following has the same answer as 27 ÷ 9?
   a. 2 × 3
   b. 6 × 3
   c. 3 × 1
   d. 9 × 3

2. There are 10 seeds in the package. If 5 seeds are used for each flower pot, how many pots are needed to plant all of the seeds?
   a. 20
   b. 19
   c. 21
   d. 2

3. Marie plants 10 rows of flowers. She plants 3 flowers in each row. Which of the following would you use to find how many flowers are in Marie's garden?
   a. 3 + 10
   b. 3 × 10
   c. 10 ÷ 3
   d. 10 − 3

4. Charles has written 7 sentences for homework. If each sentence contains 8 words, how many total words has he written?
   a. 15
   b. 1
   c. 63
   d. 56

5. Which number is even?
   a. 29
   b. 36
   c. 3
   d. 11

6. Which of the following is a solution to this problem?
   15 ÷ 3
   a. 5
   b. 12
   c. 18
   d. 6

7. If each column contains 3 words, how many columns contain 18 words?
   a. 6
   b. 15
   c. 21
   d. 5

8. Which group of numbers is in order from least to greatest?
   a. 9, 2, 10, 11, 15, 16
   b. 300, 200, 100, 50, 6
   c. 3, 9, 10, 14, 16, 21
   d. 2, 1, 7, 9, 20, 17

Copyright © 1999 Contemporary Publishing Company of Raleigh, Inc.

9. Carlos pasted 3 stars on each page of his journal. If there are 27 stars in a box, how many complete (3 stars) pages can he make?
    a. 30
    b. 9
    c. 24
    d. 8

10. Eliana can make 2 shades in one hour. How many shades does she make in 8 hours?
    a. 10
    b. 6
    c. 8
    d. 16

11. Choose the model for 4 ÷ 2?
    a. ○ ○ □ ○
    b. ○ ○ ○
    c. ○ □ ○
    d. □ ○ □ ○

12. How many cookies should be made for 7 people if each person eats 4?
    a. 11
    b. 3
    c. 28
    d. 32

13. Greg put 20 marbles in a glass container. If he takes out 4 at a time, how many times does it take to empty the container?
    a. 24
    b. 5
    c. 16
    d. 6

14. Joy has 24 feet of ribbon. She uses 6 feet on every decoration she makes. How many decorations can she make?
    a. 30
    b. 3
    c. 5
    d. 4

15. Which of the following is odd?
    a. 1,003
    b. 6,060
    c. 5,020
    d. 5,010

16. The baseball card collectors averaged a total of 9 cards each. How many cards did 8 collectors have?
    a. 17
    b. 1
    c. 64
    d. 72

17. What are the 2 odd numbers between 20 and 24?
    a. 22, 23
    b. 21, 22
    c. 21, 23
    d. 26, 28

18. $9 \times \square = 81$
    a. 9
    b. 10
    c. 72
    d. 729

19. ◯◯◯◯◯◯◯◯ =
    a. $4 \times 2 = 8$
    b. $8 \div 2 = 4$
    c. $8 \times 2 = 16$
    d. $4 + 2 = 6$

20. Each apple tree averages 7 big apples per season. How many big apples would there be on 5 trees?
    a. 12
    b. 2
    c. 40
    d. 35

21. $9 \div 3 =$ ___.
    a. 27
    b. 3
    c. 4
    d. 2

22. $64 = \square \times 8$
    a. 7
    b. 8
    c. 56
    d. 72

23. It takes 5 apples to make a pie. How many pies can you make with 40 apples?
    a. 45
    b. 8
    c. 35
    d. 9

24. $6 \times 7 =$ ___.
    a. 42
    b. 35
    c. 13
    d. 56

25. How many pieces of 5 inch cord can be cut from 25 inches?
    a. 20
    b. 6
    c. 5
    d. 30

26. $49 \div \square = 7$
    a. 3
    b. 7
    c. 8
    d. 343

27. ☐ × 7 = 35
    a. 4
    b. 3
    c. 5
    d. 245

28. 12 × 12 = ☐
    a. 1
    b. 144
    c. 24
    d. 110

CHAPTER 2

Money

COUNTING MONEY

 = quarter 25¢ or $.25

 = nickel 5¢ or $.05

 = dime 10¢ or $.10

 = penny 1¢ or $.01

EXAMPLE

How many cents equal the coins shown above?

quarter	25¢
quarter	25¢
dime	10¢
dime	10¢
penny	1¢
TOTAL	71¢

Copyright © 1999 Contemporary Publishing Company of Raleigh, Inc.

PRACTICE

Answer each of the following by counting the amount of cents for each group of coins.

1.  _____

2.  _____

3.  _____

4.  _____

5. _____

Copyright © 1999 Contemporary Publishing Company of Raleigh, Inc.

6.  _____

7.  _____

8.  _____

9.  _____

10.  _____

(continued on next page)

11.  _____

12.  _____

13.  _____

14.  _____

15. _____

16. penny penny nickel nickel _____

17. nickel nickel dime penny _____

18. penny penny quarter nickel penny _____

19. quarter penny dime nickel dime _____

20. quarter quarter nickel nickel dime _____

WRITING MONEY

EXAMPLES

$1,123.50

1. Underline the groups of numbers separated by commas or decimal.
2. The decimal is written "and."
3. The number after the decimal is written with cents after it.
4. The number to the left of the decimal is written with dollars after it.

- One thousand, one hundred twenty-three dollars and fifty cents

Two hundred twenty dollars and forty-seven cents

1. Underline the number words.
2. "And" is the decimal point.
3. Write the numbers in standard form.
4. Write in decimal point and add dollar sign.

- $220.47

PRACTICE

Write each amount in words.

1. $300.50 _____

2. $2,135.71 _____

3. $11.29 _____

4. $5,132.03 _____

5. $8,175.13 _____

6. $512.78 _____

7. $6,144.29 _____

8. $7,000.10 _____

9. $25.99 _____

10. $15.16 _____

11. $4,321.95 _____

12. $1,892.08 _____

13. $759.59 _____

14. $4,921.94 _____

15. $1,000.82 _____

Write each in money form.

16. two thousand dollars and forty cents

_____

17. ninety-five dollars and forty cents

_____

18. seven thousand dollars and ten cents

_____

19. eight hundred nineteen dollars and thirty-seven cents

_____

20. one hundred dollars and twenty-five cents

_____

21. five hundred dollars and ninety-nine cents

_____

(continued on next page)

22. seven thousand dollars and fifteen cents

_____

23. four hundred dollars and two cents

_____

24. eighty-three dollars and fifteen cents

_____

25. five hundred dollars and seventy-five cents

_____

26. six thousand dollars and ninety-nine cents

_____

27. twenty-three dollars and five cents

_____

28. nine thousand dollars and ninety-nine cents

_____

29. five dollars and thirty-three cents

_____

30. one hundred dollars and twenty cents

_____

FINDING CHANGE

Change is the money you receive from a cashier when paying for items with a larger amount than is owed.

EXAMPLES

Sweater	Cashier Receives	Change
$29.50	$40.00 (2 twenties)	?

Savannah bought a sweater that costs $29.50. She gave the cashier two twenty dollar bills. How much change would she receive?

$40.00   – $29.50   = $10.50

amount given cashier – sweater amount = change

Coat $51.00	Tax	Cashier Receives	Change
Belt $25.25	$7.80	$100.00	?

Patrick bought a new coat for $51.00 and a belt for $25.25. The tax on these two items was $7.80. If he gave the cashier a hundred dollar bill, how much change does he receive?

Add all items and tax together.

$51.00 + $25.25 + $7.80 = $84.05
  coat   belt   tax   total

Subtract total from amount given to cashier.

$100.00 – $84.05 = $15.95
  cashier   total   change
  receives

PRACTICE

Find the amount of change to be received.

Items	Amount given to cashier	Change
1. $23.95 $9.25 $1.40	$40.00	_____
2. $5.95 $2.43 $.50	$10.00	_____
3. $35.00 $18.73 $95.00	$150.00	_____
4. $7.50 $4.19 $.53 $1.21	$20.00	_____
5. $123.75 $55.61 $3.98	$200.00	_____
6. $10.00 $2.37 $1.93 $5.56	$20.00	_____
7. $90.00 $100.00 $99.95	$300.00	_____
8. $29.95 $58.75 $36.81 $18.88	$150.00	_____
9. $2,000.00 $1,000.43 $19.24	$3,020.00	_____

Copyright © 1999 Contemporary Publishing Company of Raleigh, Inc.

Items	Amount given to cashier	Change
10. $.75 $.21 $.56 $.92 $.33 $.14	$3.00	_____
11. $7.98 $12.23 $23.65 $18.93 $19.44	$100.00	_____
12. $11.24 $9.11 $3.36 $4.45	$30.00	_____
13. $150.00 $321.00 $563.00 $137.18	$1,200.00	_____
14. $1.20 $.86 $.71 $5.43 $5.18	$15.00	_____
15. $45.00 $21.00 $36.51 $41.36	$150.90	_____

Copyright © 1999 Contemporary Publishing Company of Raleigh, Inc.

ROUNDING MONEY

Money is written in hundredths since there are 100 pennies in a dollar.

$50.36 $8.07 $10.20

To round money to the nearest dollar, you must round to the nearest whole number.

EXAMPLE

$51.56 = $52.00

To round to the nearest dollar (whole number), look at the cents. 0–$.49 makes the amount of the dollar stay the same. $.50–$.99 makes the dollar go up one. $.56 makes the dollar go up one. Change the number in the cents places to zeroes.

PRACTICE

Round each to the nearest dollar.

1. $1.95 _____
2. $34.06 _____
3. $34.98 _____
4. $5.88 _____
5. $1,000.87 _____
6. $73.13 _____
7. $80.07 _____
8. $14.30 _____
9. $201.12 _____
10. $124.01 _____

11. $.99 _____
12. $10.14 _____
13. $.95 _____
14. $806.19 _____
15. $145.89 _____
16. $313.99 _____
17. $456.09 _____
18. $1.99 _____
19. $7.14 _____
20. $705.07 _____

Copyright © 1999 Contemporary Publishing Company of Raleigh, Inc.

REVIEW

1. Sydney earns $7.23 per hour. How much does he earn rounded to the nearest dollar?
   a. $7.00
   b. $72.00
   c. $8.00
   d. $73.00

2. Marjorie bought ribbon. Each yard cost $.64. How much did she pay for the ribbon to the nearest dollar?
   a. $6.40
   b. $6.00
   c. $64.00
   d. $1.00

3. Hamburger costs $1.99 per pound. How much is this per pound rounded to the nearest dollar?
   a. $1.00
   b. $2.00
   c. $19.00
   d. $20.00

4. Juice costs $2.34 per can. How much would you pay to the nearest dollar for a can of juice?
   a. $24.00
   b. $23.00
   c. $3.00
   d. $2.00

5. Warren makes $8.45 per hour. How much does he make rounded to the nearest dollar?
   a. $8.50
   b. $9.00
   c. $8.00
   d. $80.00

6. Lemons cost $1.50 per pound. How much would you pay for a pound of lemons rounded to the nearest dollar?
   a. $1.00
   b. $2.00
   c. $15.00
   d. $1.75

7. Arthur bought shares of stock at $10.36 a share. How much did he pay for a share rounded to the nearest dollar?
   a. $13.00
   b. $11.00
   c. $10.00
   d. $103.00

8. If a bicycle costs $171.99, how much would you pay for this bicycle rounded to the nearest dollar?
   a. $171.00
   b. $17.00
   c. $18.00
   d. $172.00

9. If total purchases are $75.15, what is paid rounded to the nearest dollar?
   a. $75.00
   b. $8.00
   c. $74.00
   d. $76.00

10. Bananas cost $.59 per pound. What is the cost of bananas rounded to the nearest dollar?
    a. $2.00
    b. $5.00
    c. $1.00
    d. $59.00

11. What would $73.40 be rounded to the nearest dollar?
    a. $7.00
    b. $74.00
    c. $18.00
    d. $73.00

12. Crepe costs $5.14 per yard. How much would Diana pay for the crepe rounded to the nearest dollar?
    a. $5.00
    b. $6.00
    c. $51.00
    d. $5.10

13. $1,868.34 is what rounded to the nearest dollar?
    a. $1,800.00
    b. $1,867.00
    c. $1,868.00
    d. $1,869.00

14. Erin bought a sweatshirt for $30.23, a sweater for $27.41, and a dress for $99. What were her purchases rounded to the nearest dollar?
    a. $156.00
    b. $15.00
    c. $157.00
    d. $16.00

15. Abby bought a CD for $13.99. She gave the cashier $20.00. How much change did she receive?
    a. $6.00
    b. $133.99
    c. $3.99
    d. $6.01

16. Miguel bought 5 cassettes for $60.00. How much change did he receive?
    a. $8.00
    b. $23.00
    c. not enough information given
    d. $1.00

17. Which of the following is five thousand, four hundred twenty-five dollars?
    a. $54.25
    b. $5,425.00
    c. $54,250.00
    d. $542.50

18. How do you read this amount?
    $750.01
    a. seven hundred fifty thousand, one dollars
    b. seven hundred fifty dollars and one cent
    c. seven hundred fifty million and one dollars
    d. one dollar and seven hundred fifty-one cents

19. One thousand, three hundred dollars is _____.
    a. $1,130.00
    b. $11,003.00
    c. $1,300.00
    d. $1,113.00

20. Which car is on sale for five thousand, nine hundred ninety-nine dollars?
    a. Sale: $599.00
    b. Sale: $599.99
    c. Sale: $5,999.00
    d. Sale: $5,999.99

21. $1,360.73 is _____.
    a. one thousand, three hundred sixty dollars and seventy-three cents
    b. one hundred, three hundred sixty, seventy-three dollars
    c. one hundred thirty-six, seventy-three dollars
    d. one thousand, three hundred sixty, seventy-three dollars

22. Taylor bought 6 rakes for $72 and 5 hoes for $75. How much change did he receive from $160.00?
    a. $187.00
    b. $133.00
    c. $13.00
    d. $123.00

23. How many cents equal the coins shown below?

    a. 61¢
    b. 56¢
    c. 31¢
    d. 67¢

24. Which groups show the same amount of money?

#1 (5 nickels)

#2 (2 quarters)

#3 (4 dimes and 1 nickel)

#4 (5 dimes)

a. #2 and #4
b. #3 and #4
c. #1 and #2
d. #2 and #3

25. Griffin has 28¢ in his pocket. Which of the following shows coins equalling 28¢?

a. (1 quarter, 2 pennies)

b. (3 dimes)

c. (3 dimes, 2 pennies)

d. (1 quarter, 3 pennies)

44

CHAPTER 3

FRACTIONS

REPRESENTING FRACTIONS

EXAMPLES

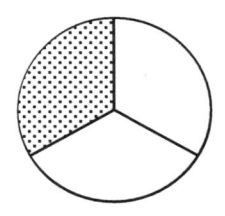

$\frac{1}{3}$

1 = number of pieces shaded
3 = total parts figure is divided into

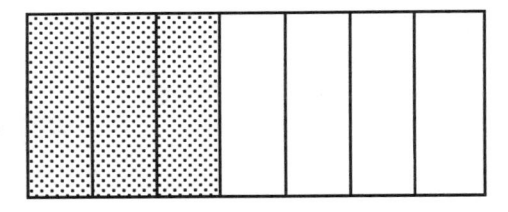

$\frac{3}{7}$

3 = number of pieces shaded
7 = total parts figure is divided into

PRACTICE

Draw a figure to represent each fraction.

1. $\dfrac{1}{2}$

2. $\dfrac{3}{10}$

3. $\dfrac{3}{8}$

4. $\dfrac{1}{3}$

5. $\dfrac{2}{5}$

6. $\dfrac{1}{9}$

7. $\dfrac{2}{4}$

8. $\dfrac{3}{6}$

9. $\dfrac{3}{4}$

10. $\dfrac{2}{3}$

11. $\dfrac{1}{6}$

12. $\dfrac{5}{7}$

13. $\dfrac{1}{10}$

14. $\dfrac{5}{6}$

15. $\dfrac{1}{7}$

16. $\dfrac{9}{10}$

17. $\dfrac{8}{9}$

18. $\dfrac{1}{4}$

19. $\dfrac{3}{9}$

20. $\dfrac{2}{10}$

(continued on next page)

Write the fraction that is represented by each figure.

21.

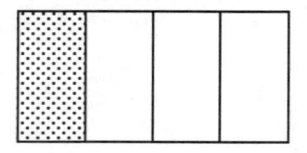

22.

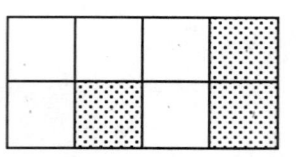

23.

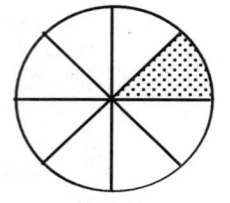

24.

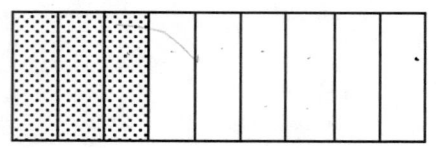

25.

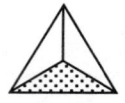

26.

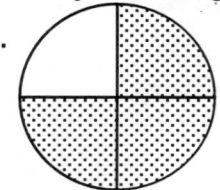

27.

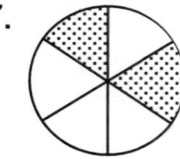

28.

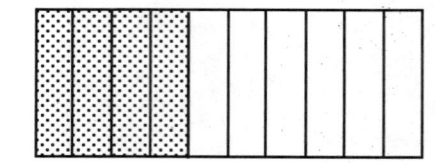

29.

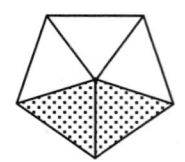

30.

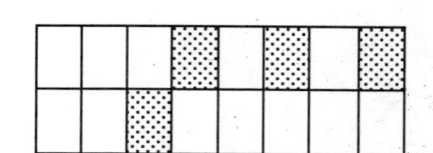

REPRESENTING MIXED NUMBERS

EXAMPLES

$= 1\frac{1}{4}$

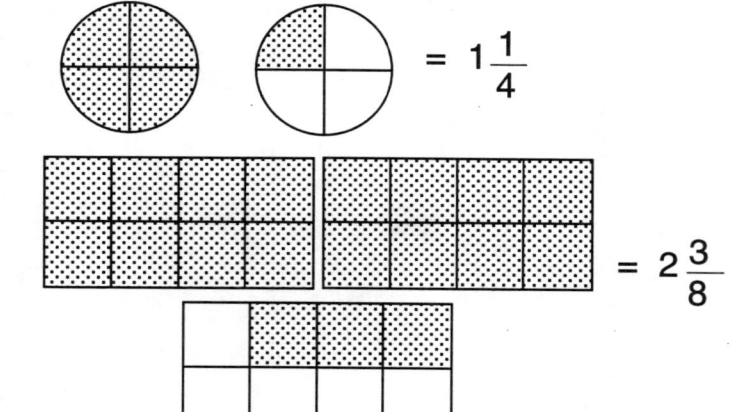

$= 2\frac{3}{8}$

PRACTICE

Draw figures to represent each mixed number.

1. $2\frac{1}{3}$

2. $1\frac{4}{5}$

3. $1\frac{1}{8}$

4. $2\frac{3}{4}$

5. $3\frac{1}{2}$

6. $1\frac{1}{10}$

7. $2\frac{4}{7}$

8. $3\frac{3}{8}$

9. $1\frac{2}{3}$

10. $2\frac{4}{9}$

(continued on next page)

Write the mixed number that each figure represents.

11. _____

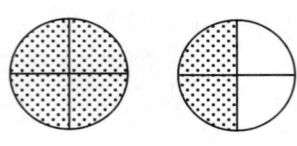

12. _____

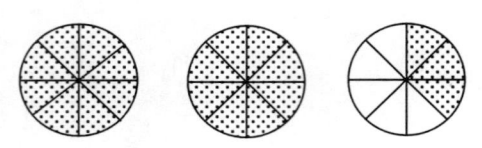

13. _____

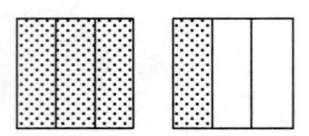

14. _____

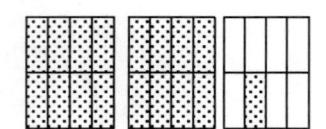

15. _____

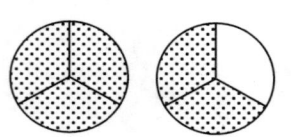

16. _____

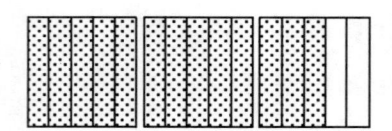

17. _____

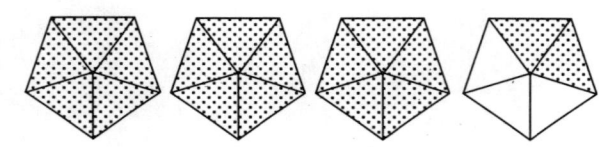

18. _____

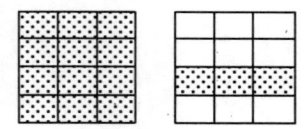

19. _____

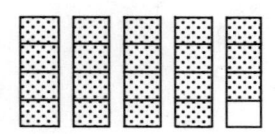

20. _____

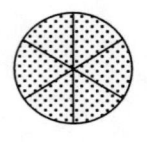

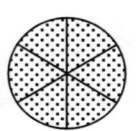

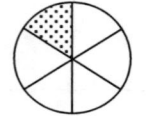

50

Copyright © 1999 Contemporary Publishing Company of Raleigh, Inc.

ORDERING FRACTIONS

Ordering fractions is to put fractions in a certain sequence (larger to smaller, smaller to larger).

EXAMPLE
Write these fractions in order from smallest to largest.

$$\frac{1}{7}, \frac{6}{7}, \frac{4}{7}, \frac{3}{7}$$

Since all of these fractions have the denominator (bottom number) of 7, you just order by the top number (numerator).

$$\frac{1}{7}, \frac{3}{7}, \frac{4}{7}, \frac{6}{7}$$

EXAMPLE
Write these fractions in order from largest to smallest. $\frac{1}{4}, \frac{1}{8}, \frac{1}{3}$

In fractions, the larger the denominator, the smaller the fraction.

Since all numerators are one, put the denominators in order from smallest number to largest number.

$$\frac{1}{3}, \frac{1}{4}, \frac{1}{8}$$

PRACTICE

Put each group of fractions in order from smallest to largest.

1. $\frac{3}{9}, \frac{2}{9}, \frac{7}{9}$ _____
2. $\frac{3}{8}, \frac{1}{8}, \frac{2}{8}$ _____
3. $\frac{9}{10}, \frac{4}{10}, \frac{1}{10}$ _____
4. $\frac{3}{4}, \frac{1}{4}, \frac{2}{4}$ _____
5. $\frac{10}{11}, \frac{9}{11}, \frac{1}{11}$ _____
6. $\frac{1}{7}, \frac{6}{7}, \frac{2}{7}$ _____
7. $\frac{2}{3}, \frac{1}{3}, \frac{3}{3}$ _____

8. $\frac{12}{13}, \frac{10}{13}, \frac{9}{13}$ _____
9. $\frac{1}{2}, \frac{1}{4}, \frac{1}{9}$ _____
10. $\frac{1}{2}, \frac{1}{7}, \frac{1}{5}$ _____
11. $\frac{1}{8}, \frac{1}{5}, \frac{1}{4}$ _____
12. $\frac{1}{2}, \frac{1}{8}, \frac{1}{4}$ _____
13. $\frac{1}{2}, \frac{1}{5}, \frac{1}{10}$ _____
14. $\frac{1}{6}, \frac{1}{2}, \frac{1}{4}$ _____

Put each group of fractions in order from largest to smallest.

15. $\frac{3}{13}, \frac{9}{13}, \frac{1}{13}$ _____
16. $\frac{4}{5}, \frac{1}{5}, \frac{3}{5}$ _____
17. $\frac{9}{11}, \frac{8}{11}, \frac{1}{11}$ _____
18. $\frac{4}{6}, \frac{5}{6}, \frac{6}{6}$ _____
19. $\frac{1}{15}, \frac{4}{15}, \frac{2}{15}$ _____
20. $\frac{1}{5}, \frac{1}{8}, \frac{1}{2}$ _____
21. $\frac{1}{3}, \frac{1}{8}, \frac{1}{6}$ _____

22. $\frac{1}{2}, \frac{1}{4}, \frac{1}{3}$ _____
23. $\frac{1}{4}, \frac{1}{3}, \frac{1}{6}$ _____
24. $\frac{1}{8}, \frac{1}{2}, \frac{1}{4}$ _____
25. $\frac{1}{9}, \frac{1}{4}, \frac{1}{3}$ _____
26. $\frac{1}{2}, \frac{1}{8}, \frac{1}{7}$ _____
27. $\frac{1}{4}, \frac{1}{3}, \frac{1}{8}$ _____
28. $\frac{1}{5}, \frac{1}{4}, \frac{1}{3}$ _____

EQUIVALENT FRACTIONS

Equivalent fractions are fractions that represent the same amount.

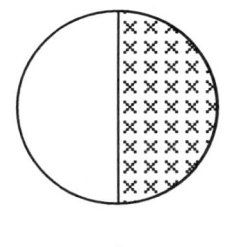

$\frac{1}{2}$ 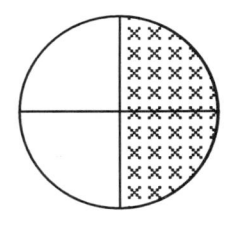 $\frac{2}{4}$ 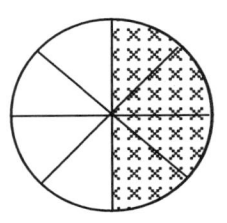 $\frac{4}{8}$

$\frac{1}{2}, \frac{2}{4}$ and $\frac{4}{8}$ are equivalent fractions.

Equivalent fractions are found by multiplying or dividing the numerator (top number) and the denominator (bottom number) by the same number.

EXAMPLES

$\frac{6 \div 2}{8 \div 2} = \frac{3}{4}$ $\frac{6}{8}$ and $\frac{3}{4}$ are equivalent.

$\frac{6 \times 2}{8 \times 2} = \frac{12}{16}$ $\frac{6}{8}$ and $\frac{12}{16}$ are equivalent.

$\frac{3}{4}, \frac{6}{8}$ and $\frac{12}{16}$ are equivalent fractions.

PRACTICE

Write an equivalent fraction for each of the following.

1. $\frac{2}{16}$ _____
2. $\frac{1}{3}$ _____
3. $\frac{2}{6}$ _____
4. $\frac{1}{6}$ _____
5. $\frac{8}{24}$ _____
6. $\frac{8}{11}$ _____
7. $\frac{1}{9}$ _____
8. $\frac{3}{5}$ _____
9. $\frac{2}{3}$ _____
10. $\frac{10}{12}$ _____

11. $\frac{9}{10}$ _____
12. $\frac{3}{6}$ _____
13. $\frac{8}{18}$ _____
14. $\frac{1}{7}$ _____
15. $\frac{1}{5}$ _____
16. $\frac{5}{7}$ _____
17. $\frac{1}{10}$ _____
18. $\frac{2}{8}$ _____
19. $\frac{11}{12}$ _____
20. $\frac{5}{6}$ _____

ADDITION OF FRACTIONS WITH LIKE DENOMINATORS

To add fractions with like denominators, write down the denominator. Add the top numbers (numerators). Reduce if necessary.

EXAMPLES AND MODELS

$$\frac{5}{8} + \frac{2}{8} = \frac{7}{8}$$

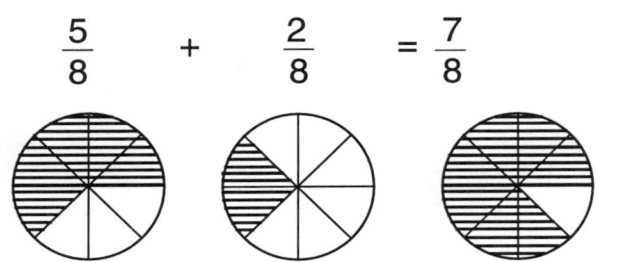

$$\frac{1}{3} + \frac{1}{3} = \frac{2}{3}$$

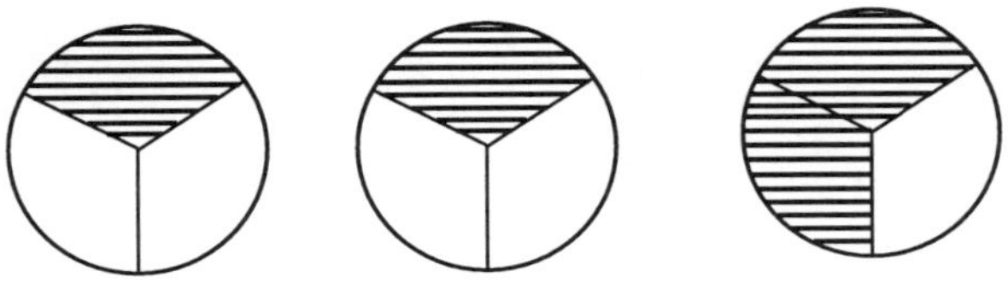

$$1\frac{1}{4} + \frac{2}{4} = 1\frac{3}{4}$$

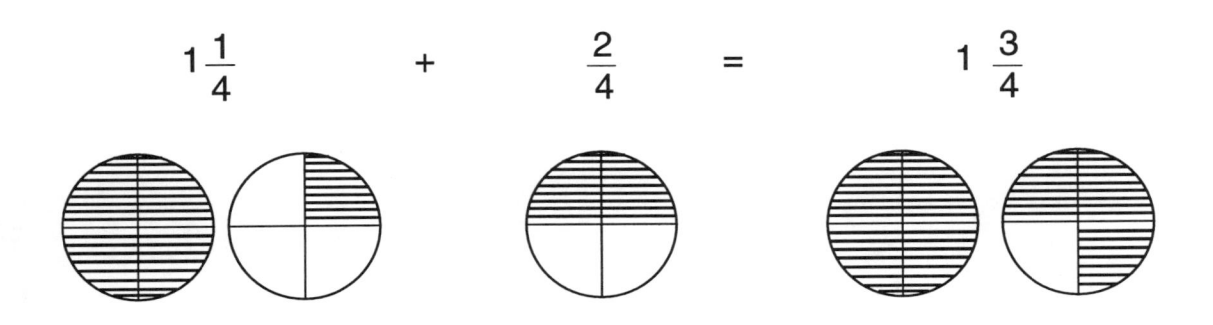

PRACTICE

Add. Model *'d problems.

*1. $\dfrac{1}{3} + \dfrac{1}{3}$

*6. $\dfrac{7}{15} + \dfrac{1}{15}$

*11. $\dfrac{3}{10} + \dfrac{4}{10}$

*2. $\dfrac{2}{5} + \dfrac{1}{5}$

7. $3\dfrac{4}{9} + \dfrac{1}{9}$

12. $3\dfrac{1}{8} + 2\dfrac{1}{8}$

*3. $\dfrac{2}{9} + \dfrac{5}{9}$

8. $18\dfrac{1}{6} + 19\dfrac{4}{6}$

13. $124\dfrac{3}{5} + 26\dfrac{1}{5}$

*4. $\dfrac{6}{11} + \dfrac{4}{11}$

9. $25\dfrac{4}{7} + 37\dfrac{1}{7}$

14. $70\dfrac{7}{12} + \dfrac{4}{12}$

*5. $\dfrac{9}{16} + \dfrac{2}{16}$

10. $121\dfrac{5}{7} + 9\dfrac{1}{7}$

*15. $\dfrac{5}{12} + \dfrac{2}{12}$

Copyright © 1999 Contemporary Publishing Company of Raleigh, Inc.

SUBTRACTING FRACTIONS

To subtract fractions with like denominators, write down the denominator. Subtract the top numbers (numerators). Reduce if necessary.

EXAMPLES AND MODELS

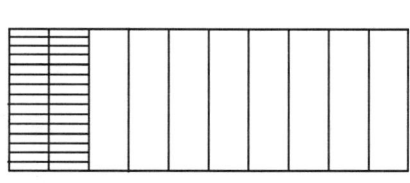

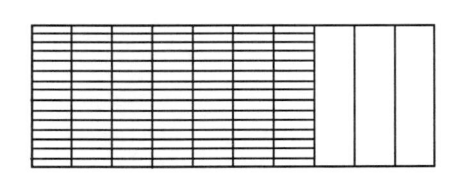

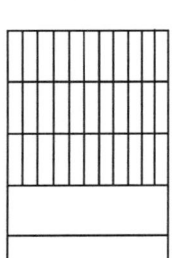

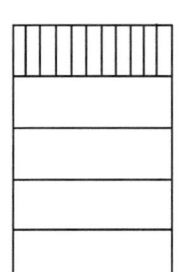

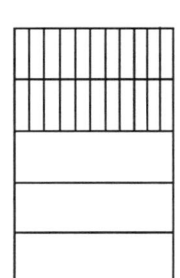

$$\frac{9}{10} - \frac{2}{10} = \frac{7}{10}$$

$$\frac{3}{5} - \frac{1}{5} = \frac{2}{5}$$

When subtracting mixed numbers with like denominators, subtract the fractions first, then subtract the whole numbers. Reduce if necessary.

EXAMPLES

$$10\frac{3}{4} - 8\frac{2}{4} = 2\frac{1}{4}$$

$$\overset{3}{\cancel{4}}\overset{15}{\cancel{5}}\frac{11}{12} - 19\frac{4}{12} = 26\frac{7}{12}$$

Copyright © 1999 Contemporary Publishing Company of Raleigh, Inc.

PRACTICE

Subtract. Draw models for *'d problems.

*1. $\dfrac{4}{7} - \dfrac{3}{7}$

6. $\dfrac{25}{28} - \dfrac{2}{28}$

*11. $\dfrac{8}{9} - \dfrac{1}{9}$

*2. $\dfrac{19}{20} - \dfrac{16}{20}$

7. $\dfrac{26}{27} - \dfrac{3}{27}$

*12. $\dfrac{11}{12} - \dfrac{4}{12}$

*3. $\dfrac{10}{11} - \dfrac{3}{11}$

8. $30\dfrac{3}{4} - 14\dfrac{2}{4}$

13. $200\dfrac{14}{15} - 19\dfrac{10}{15}$

4. $703\dfrac{9}{10} - 140\dfrac{2}{10}$

9. $77\dfrac{6}{7} - 56\dfrac{2}{7}$

14. $38\dfrac{2}{3} - 19\dfrac{1}{3}$

5. $345\dfrac{13}{14} - \dfrac{10}{14}$

10. $104\dfrac{1}{2} - 14\dfrac{1}{2}$

15. $807\dfrac{7}{13} - 119\dfrac{4}{13}$

MODELING FRACTIONS

EXAMPLES

Illustrate $\frac{1}{2}$ of 6 boxes.

$\frac{1}{2} \times 6 = 3$

Illustrate $\frac{3}{5}$ of 10 boxes.

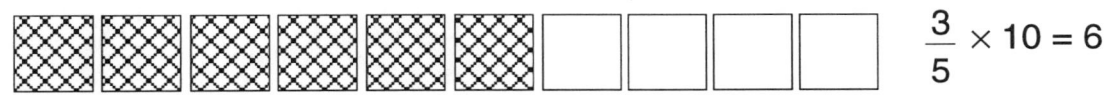

$\frac{3}{5} \times 10 = 6$

Illustrate $\frac{2}{3}$ of $\frac{1}{3}$.

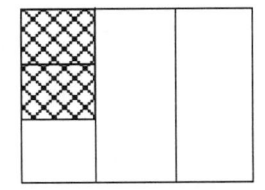

59

PRACTICE

Illustrate each of the following.

1. $\frac{1}{3}$ of 9 boxes

2. $\frac{1}{2}$ of $\frac{3}{4}$

3. $\frac{2}{3}$ of $\frac{1}{2}$

4. $\frac{1}{8}$ of 8 boxes

5. $\frac{2}{5}$ of 10 triangles

6. $\frac{1}{2}$ of 4 squares

7. $\frac{3}{4}$ of 1 circle

8. $\frac{1}{8}$ of $\frac{1}{2}$

REVIEW

1. Which fraction is equivalent to $\frac{1}{2}$?
   a. $\frac{16}{32}$
   b. $\frac{6}{8}$
   c. $\frac{12}{15}$
   d. $\frac{9}{12}$

2. Which figure represents $\frac{1}{2}$?
   a. 
   b. 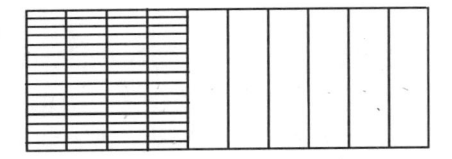
   c. 
   d.

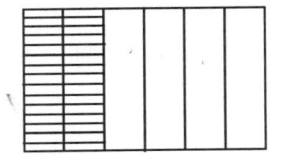

3. =
   a. $3\frac{3}{4}$
   b. $2\frac{1}{4}$
   c. $1\frac{3}{4}$
   d. $2\frac{3}{4}$

4. All of the following are $\frac{1}{2}$ except ___.
   a. 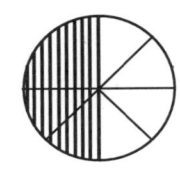
   b. 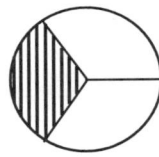
   c. 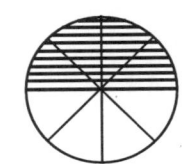
   d.

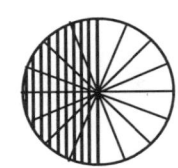

5. Which fraction is smaller than $\frac{1}{2}$?
   a. $\frac{1}{4}$
   b. $\frac{4}{8}$
   c. $\frac{6}{12}$
   d. $\frac{7}{14}$

6. Which fraction is larger than $\frac{1}{2}$?

   a. $\frac{1}{6}$

   b. $\frac{3}{4}$

   c. $\frac{2}{4}$

   d. $\frac{1}{10}$

7. $3\frac{3}{4} - 1\frac{2}{4} =$ _____.

   a. $4\frac{5}{4}$

   b. $2\frac{1}{4}$

   c. $1\frac{1}{4}$

   d. $2\frac{2}{4}$

8. 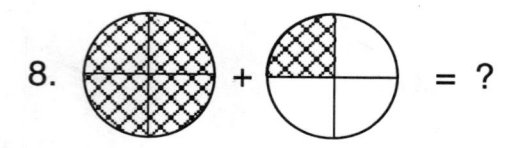 ⊗ + ⊘ = ?

   a. $2\frac{1}{2}$

   b. $1\frac{3}{4}$

   c. $1\frac{1}{4}$

   d. $5\frac{3}{4}$

9. What is the solution to the following?

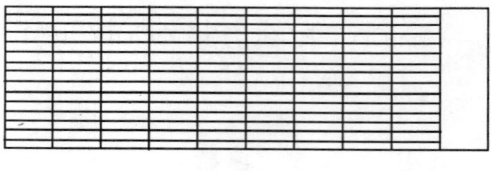

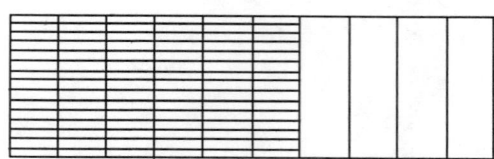

   a. $\frac{7}{10}$

   b. $\frac{1}{10}$

   c. $\frac{2}{5}$

   d. $\frac{3}{10}$

10. Joe bought 3 ½ pounds of taffy and 4 ½ pounds of peanut brittle for his classmates. What expression would you use to find the total pounds Joe bought?

    a. $4\frac{1}{2} - 3\frac{1}{2}$

    b. $4\frac{1}{2} \times 3\frac{1}{2}$

    c. $4\frac{1}{2} \div 3\frac{1}{2}$

    d. $4\frac{1}{2} + 3\frac{1}{2}$

11. The subway traveled 16 ¼ miles north, 5 ¼ miles east, and 4 ¼ miles south. What was the total miles traveled?

   a. $25\frac{0}{4}$

   b. $25\frac{3}{4}$

   c. $25\frac{3}{12}$

   d. $25\frac{1}{4}$

12. $3\frac{1}{4}$ = _____.

   a.

   b.

   c.

   d.

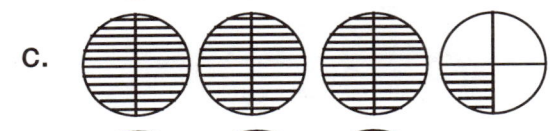

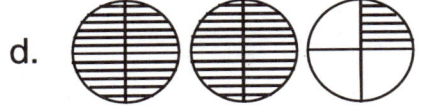

13. If the shaded portion is removed, how much of the original circle is left?

   a. $\frac{3}{8}$

   b. $\frac{8}{8} = 1$

   c. $\frac{1}{2}$

   d. $\frac{5}{8}$

14. Which model represents $1\frac{3}{4}$?

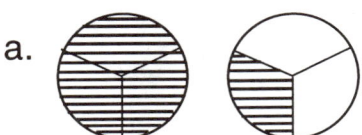

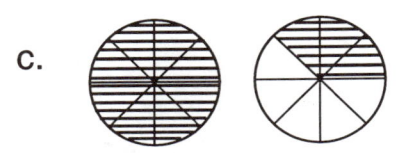

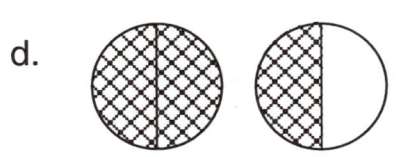

   a.

   b.

   c.

   d.

15. $\frac{3}{4}$ is equivalent to _____.

   a. $\frac{1}{2}$

   b. $\frac{9}{15}$

   c. $\frac{36}{48}$

   d. $\frac{9}{16}$

16. $\frac{3}{8} + \frac{4}{8}$ = _____.

   a. $\frac{7}{16}$

   b. $\frac{1}{16}$

   c. $\frac{7}{0}$

   d. $\frac{7}{8}$

Copyright © 1999 Contemporary Publishing Company of Raleigh, Inc.

17. $\frac{5}{6} - \frac{4}{6} =$ _____.

   a. $\frac{9}{6}$
   b. $\frac{1}{0}$
   c. $\frac{2}{6}$
   d. $\frac{1}{6}$

18. Vickie can read the comics in 11 ½ minutes. Her brother can read the same comics in 10 ½ minutes. How much longer does it take Vickie to read the comics?

   a. $\frac{3}{4}$ min.
   b. 1 $\frac{1}{4}$ min.
   c. 1 min.
   d. 1 $\frac{3}{8}$ min.

19. Nasir works 6 2/4 hours on Saturday, 3 1/4 hours on Sunday, and 12 hours on Monday. How many total hours did he work?

   a. 21 $\frac{2}{4}$ hrs.
   b. 21 $\frac{1}{8}$ hrs.
   c. 21 $\frac{3}{8}$ hrs.
   d. 21 $\frac{3}{4}$ hrs.

20. Which group of fractions is listed in order from smallest to largest?

   a. $\frac{1}{7}, \frac{1}{4}, \frac{1}{3}, \frac{1}{2}$
   b. $\frac{1}{2}, \frac{1}{8}, \frac{1}{10}, \frac{1}{11}$
   c. $\frac{3}{11}, \frac{2}{11}, \frac{1}{11}, \frac{10}{11}$
   d. $\frac{4}{12}, \frac{5}{12}, \frac{1}{12}, \frac{4}{9}$

21. Which problem does the shaded part of the picture represent?

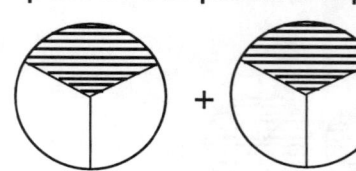

   a. $\frac{2}{3} + \frac{2}{3} = \frac{4}{3}$
   b. $\frac{1}{3} + \frac{1}{3} = \frac{2}{3}$
   c. $\frac{1}{3} + \frac{2}{3} = \frac{3}{3}$
   d. $\frac{1}{3} - \frac{1}{3} = 0$

22. Which illustration represents ½ of ¼?

   a. 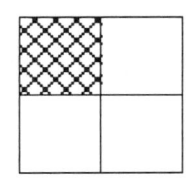

   b. 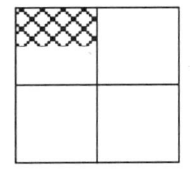

   c. 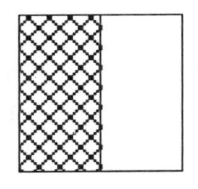

   d.

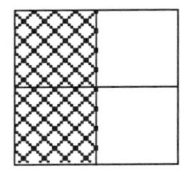

23. In which figure is the fraction of the shaded area the least?

   a. 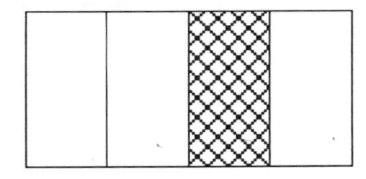

   b. 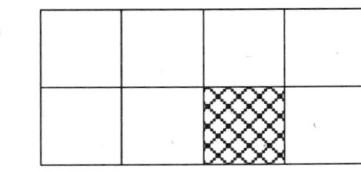

   c. 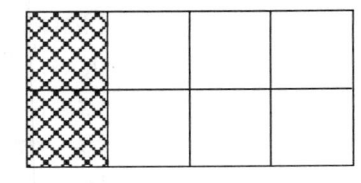

   d.

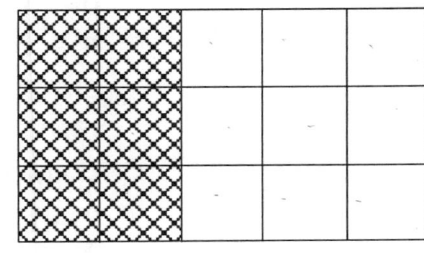

Copyright © 1999 Contemporary Publishing Company of Raleigh, Inc.

CHAPTER 4

ESTIMATING

ROUNDING

Numbers can be rounded to the nearest ten, hundred, thousand, etc. to help us estimate answers to problems.

EXAMPLES

17<u>6</u>|5 = 1,770

Round to the nearest ten. Find the tens place and underline. Draw a line to separate tens place from ones place. Look at the number to the right of the line. This number determines if the 6 goes up or stays the same. (If the number is between 0-4, the 6 remains a 6. If the number is 5-9, the 6 goes up one to 7.) Since the number is 5, the 6 changes to a 7. Write down the 17, change 6 to 7, and replace all numbers after the line with zeroes.

3<u>8</u>|41 = 3,800

Round to nearest hundred. A 4 is to the right of the line, so there is no change. Write 38 (since no change) and 00 to replace numbers after line.

PRACTICE

Round to the nearest ten.			
1. 87 _____	6. 2,678 _____	11. 56 _____	16. 94 _____
2. 390 _____	7. 1,002 _____	12. 123 _____	17. 836 _____
3. 245 _____	8. 517 _____	13. 4,802 _____	18. 9,412 _____
4. 657 _____	9. 8,962 _____	14. 5,076 _____	19. 3,007 _____
5. 1,391 _____	10. 347 _____	15. 1,450 _____	20. 840 _____

Copyright © 1999 Contemporary Publishing Company of Raleigh, Inc.

Round to the nearest hundred.

1. 396 _____
2. 1,407 _____
3. 245 _____
4. 657 _____
5. 8,889 _____

6. 456 _____
7. 1,243 _____
8. 517 _____
9. 8,962 _____
10. 5,789 _____

11. 4,567 _____
12. 320 _____
13. 4,802 _____
14. 5,076 _____
15. 344 _____

16. 9,373 _____
17. 836 _____
18. 9,412 _____
19. 1,345 _____
20. 888 _____

Round to the nearest thousand.

1. 8,069 _____
2. 9,998 _____
3. 5,176 _____
4. 8,545 _____
5. 1,056 _____

6. 5,662 _____
7. 1,035 _____
8. 16,545 _____
9. 89,312 _____
10. 64,512 _____

11. 81,234 _____
12. 99,863 _____
13. 34,512 _____
14. 81,736 _____
15. 21,374 _____

16. 11,214 _____
17. 8,960 _____
18. 3,403 _____
19. 79,343 _____
20. 8,888 _____

ESTIMATING

Rounding is used for estimating answers. You can get an approximate answer by estimating.

EXAMPLES

Estimate the sum.   386 + 295 + 65 + 307 =
400 + 300 + 70 + 300 = 1070 estimate
(Round to largest place value.)

Estimate the difference.   3,864 − 465 =
4000 − 500 = 3,500 estimate
(Round to the largest place value.)

PRACTICE

Estimate the answer for each problem.

1. 78 + 193 + 65

2. 129 + 4,861 + 294

3. 37 + 189 + 1,556

4. 3,945 − 214

5. 8,645 − 3,845

6. 2,014 − 38

7. 1,875 − 914

8. 567 − 89

9. 45 + 31

10. 29 + 50

11. 73 − 21

12. 295 + 35

13. 317 − 24

14. 1,996 + 561

15. 120 − 58

16. 87 + 15 + 25

17. 3,450 − 2,013

18. 850 + 674

19. 37 + 81

20. 43 + 891

REVIEW

1. Paula made a list of the items she needs to purchase this month.

Nail Polish	$3.75
Mascara	$1.50
Pencils	$.75
Pen	$2.19

   What is the *best* way for her to estimate the amount of money she will need?
   a. Multiply the highest price by 2.
   b. Multiply the middle price by 4.
   c. Round each item to the nearest cent and add.
   d. Round each item to the nearest dollar and add.

2. Jennifer bought a necklace for $27.75 and earrings for $18.20. *About* how much change would she receive from a $50 bill?
   a. $4, because 50 − (28 + 18) = 4.
   b. $5, because 50 − (27 + 18) = 5.
   c. $3, because 50 − (28 + 19) = 3.
   d. $2, because 50 − (29 + 19) = 2.

3. Gary drives 3.5 miles to Bud's house, goes back home, drives 2.1 miles to the church, and then returns home. *About* how many miles did he drive today?
   a. 5.6 miles, because 3.5 + 2.1 = 5.6.
   b. 6 miles, because 4 + 2 = 6.
   c. 12 miles, because (4 + 2) × 2 = 12.
   d. 14 miles, because (4 + 3) × 2 = 14.

4. Which of the following would not need an exact answer?
   a. If Mike gave the cashier $75 to pay for a $37.85 shirt, how much change would he receive?
   b. Catherine has $5.00. Does she have enough money to buy chicken nuggets for $2.87, a cola for $.75, and an ice cream cone for $.99?
   c. How much does Tarra earn if she works 15 hours and is paid $7.25 per hour?
   d. Alex paid for groceries that cost $75.85 with 4 twenty dollar bills. He received $3 in change. Is this correct?

5. 325 students have CD players in the fourth grade. What is the best estimate of how many students have CD players?
   a. 3,000 students
   b. 200 students
   c. 400 students
   d. 300 students

6. To the nearest dollar, estimate how much money Stan spent at the sports shop.

$15.61	socks
$33.18	basketball
$23.95	T-shirt

   a. $71
   b. $73
   c. $72.74
   d. $74

7. Which expression would you use to estimate 144 – 23?
   a. 150 – 20
   b. 140 – 30
   c. 140 – 20
   d. 150 – 30

8. Robert earns $7,562 per month. What is the best estimate of his monthly income?
   a. $6,000
   b. $7,000
   c. $8,000
   d. $9,000

9. Janice earned $175, $243, $794, and $856 from her part time job. What is the estimate of her earnings?
   a. $2,100
   b. $2,068
   c. $1,200
   d. $2,800

10. What expression would you use to find the estimate of Janice's earnings in problem #9 rounded to the nearest ten?
    a. $200 + $200 + $800 + $900
    b. $170 + $240 + $790 + $850
    c. $100 + $200 + $800 + $900
    d. $180 + $240 + $790 + $860

11. If Calvin uses 85 yards of material to make drapes, estimate the number of yards used for drapes.
    a. 90 yards
    b. 80 yards
    c. 100 yards
    d. 120 yards

12. Maria uses 21 pounds of grapes to make 1 fruit centerpiece. Estimate the number of pounds of grapes needed for 2 centerpieces.
    a. 40 lbs.
    b. 30 lbs.
    c. 20 lbs.
    d. 50 lbs.

13. The best estimate for 90 + 31 is _____.
    a. 370
    b. 430
    c. 530
    d. 460

14. Round 8,765 to the nearest hundred.
    a. 9,000
    b. 8,000
    c. 8,800
    d. 8,700

15. What is the estimated difference of 573 – 245?
    a. 200
    b. 818
    c. 328
    d. 400

16. Frank earns $495 per week. What is his estimated weekly income?
    a. $400
    b. $600
    c. $500
    d. $300

17. Round 5,963 to the nearest thousand.
    a. 5,000
    b. 5,960
    c. 6,900
    d. 6,000

18. Jane used 67 pieces of material in her baby quilt. Estimate the number of pieces used for 2 quilts.
    a. 140
    b. 100
    c. 155
    d. 200

19. Round 3,124 to the nearest ten.
    a. 3,100
    b. 3,120
    c. 3,000
    d. 3,130

20. What expression would you use to estimate 314 + 25?
    a. 400 + 20
    b. 300 + 20
    c. 300 + 30
    d. 300 + 40

21. The best estimate for 619 − 31 is ___.
    a. 470
    b. 430
    c. 630
    d. 570

22. Monique uses 11 yards of ribbon for each bow. Estimate the yards of ribbon needed for 3 bows.
    a. 50 yds.
    b. 30 yds.
    c. 15 yds.
    d. 25 yds.

23. What is the estimated difference of 113 − 48?
    a. 50
    b. 70
    c. 5
    d. 150

CHAPTER 5

NUMBER LINES

IDENTIFYING NUMBERS ON A NUMBER LINE

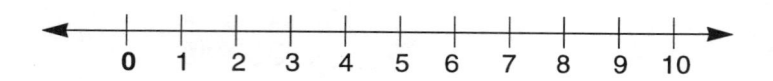

A number line contains points that represent numbers (2, 3, 4, 5. . .). Numbers to the right of zero are positive (+2, 2, 5, +5).

EXAMPLE

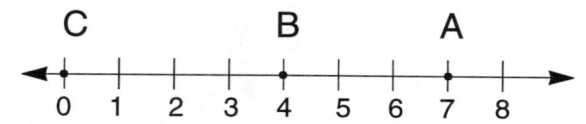

What number is point A?   7

What point is between C and A?   B

MOVING ON A NUMBER LINE

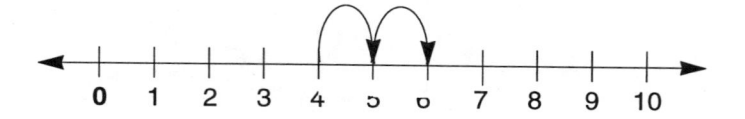

EXAMPLE

Start on 4. Move 2 units to the right. What number do you reach?   6

PRACTICE

Use the number line below to find the answer to each of the following.

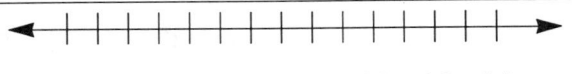

```
◄─┼─┼─┼─┼─┼─┼─┼─┼─┼─┼─┼─┼─┼─┼─►
  0   2   4   6   8  10  12  14
```

What number do you reach when you move....

1. 3 units to the right of 1? _____

2. 1 unit to the left of 7? _____

3. 7 units to the right of 0? _____

4. 1 unit to the right of 6? _____

5. 5 units to the left of 7? _____

6. 1 unit to the right of 1? _____

7. 2 units to the left of 5? _____

8. 6 units to the right of 0? _____

9. 4 units to the left of 7? _____

10. 5 units to the right of 1? _____

11. 2 units to the right of 2? _____

12. 9 units to the right of 5? _____

13. Draw a number line. Show the movement 3 units to the right of 1. What number do you reach? _____

14. Draw a number line that contains these points.
    A = 3, B = 1, C = 4, D = 0, E = 5

15. Draw a number line that contains these points.
    A = 1, B = 0, C = 3, D = 6, E = 2

16. Draw a number line that contains these points.
    A = 2, B = 3, C = 4, D = 5, E = 6, G = 7

Copyright © 1999 Contemporary Publishing Company of Raleigh, Inc.

```
A    B    C  D E    F    G H   I    J    K    L    M
<---+----+----+-+---+----+-+---+----+----+----+----+--->
0    3    6    9   12   15   18   21   24   27
```

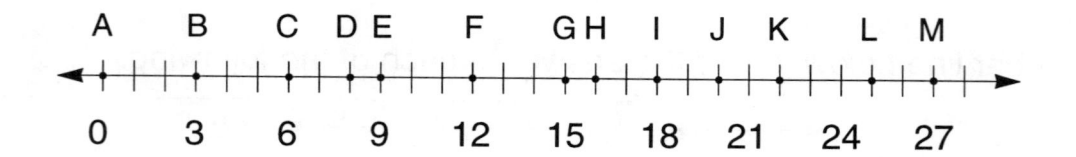

REVIEW

1. Which point represents 15?
   a. K
   b. I
   c. G
   d. C

2. What point falls between H and J?
   a. K
   b. J
   c. D
   d. I

3. What point falls between points H and F?
   a. 15
   b. 14
   c. 13
   d. 12

4. What point represents 6?
   a. H
   b. F
   c. C
   d. G

5. Which point represents 0?
   a. B
   b. M
   c. L
   d. A

6. 18 is point ___.
   a. J
   b. I
   c. E
   d. G

7. Which point has the greatest value?
   a. A
   b. F
   c. G
   d. C

8. Which point lies between 24 and 12?
   a. E
   b. J
   c. L
   d. C

9. What is the numerical value of point H?
   a. 18
   b. 17
   c. 15
   d. 16

10. Zero is greater than which point?
    a. H
    b. none of them
    c. F
    d. C

Copyright © 1999 Contemporary Publishing Company of Raleigh, Inc.

```
R   S   T   U   V   W   X   Y   Z
←●——●———●———●———●———●———●———●———●→
0   1   2   3   4   5   6   7   8
```

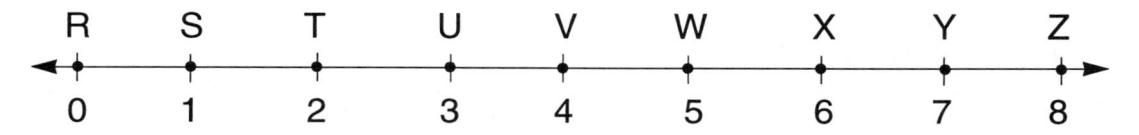

11. What is the value of Y?
    a. 1
    b. 8
    c. 6
    d. 7

12. What point falls between point S and point U?
    a. R
    b. V
    c. W
    d. T

13. What number represents point U?
    a. 4
    b. 3
    c. 2
    d. 0

14. Which point is greater than W?
    a. Y
    b. S
    c. T
    d. U

15. Point V is less than point_____.
    a. W
    b. U
    c. S
    d. R

16. What is the value of point W?
    a. 4
    b. 0
    c. 5
    d. 3

17. Which point is farthest from point V?
    a. W
    b. X
    c. Y
    d. Z

18. Which point is closest to point V?
    a. W
    b. X
    c. Y
    d. Z

19. What point falls between points U and W?
    a. X
    b. V
    c. Y
    d. Z

20. Which point represents 1?
    a. U
    b. W
    c. Y
    d. S

21. What number do you reach when you move 4 units to the right of 2?
    a. 5
    b. 6
    c. 0
    d. 1

22. What number do you reach when you move 3 units to the left of 3?
    a. 1
    b. 0
    c. 6
    d. 1

Copyright © 1999 Contemporary Publishing Company of Raleigh, Inc.

CHAPTER 6

MEASUREMENTS

STANDARD MEASUREMENTS

LENGTH:
1 foot = 12 inches
1 yard = 3 feet or 36 inches
1 mile = 1,760 yards or 5,280 feet

WEIGHT:
1 pound = 16 ounces
1 ton = 2,000 pounds

LIQUID MEASURES:
1 pint = 16 ounces or 2 cups
1 quart = 2 pints or 32 ounces
1 gallon = 4 quarts or 8 pints or 128 ounces
1 cup = 8 ounces

TIME:
1 minute = 60 seconds
1 hour = 60 minutes or 3,600 seconds
1 day = 24 hours
1 week = 7 days
1 year = 12 months or 52 weeks or 365 days

EXAMPLES

How many cups are in 2 pints?
1 pint = 2 cups
2 × 2 = 4 cups

How many seconds are in 2 minutes?
1 minute = 60 seconds
60 + 60 = 120 seconds

PRACTICE

Solve each measurement problem.

1. 5 minutes = _____ seconds

2. 2 hours 45 minutes = _____ minutes

3. 4 years = _____ days

4. 4 days = _____ hours

5. 3 weeks = _____ days

6. 2 pints = _____ ounces

7. 8 quarts = _____ pints

8. 6 gallons 2 pints = _____ pints

9. 3 quarts = _____ cups

10. 32 ounces = _____ quarts

11. 3 pounds = _____ ounces

12. 5 yards = _____ feet

13. 36 inches = _____ yards

14. 4 tons = _____ pounds

15. 12 months = _____ year(s)

16. 4 feet = _____ inches

17. 9 yards = _____ feet

18. 3 hours = _____ minutes

19. 2 miles = _____ yards

20. 3 minutes 15 seconds = _____ seconds

(continued on next page)

Which unit would you use to measure each of the following?

21. inch or foot?

22. yard or mile?

23. foot or yard?

24. cup or gallon?

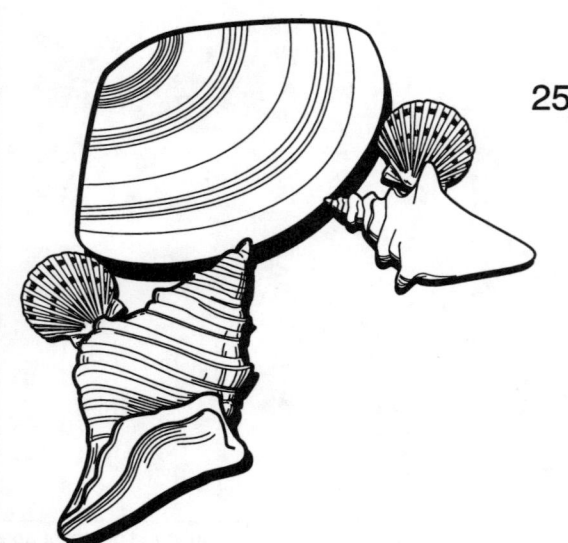

25. ounce or pound?

REVIEW

1. A jar of jam weighs 3 pounds. How many ounces is this?
   a. 24 ounces
   b. 9 ounces
   c. 48 ounces
   d. 36 ounces

2. Marceline studied for 2 hours, Hazel for 110 minutes, Leda for 65 minutes and Lee for 83 minutes. Who studied longest?
   a. Lee
   b. Leda
   c. Hazel
   d. Marceline

3. 5 yards is how many feet?
   a. 15 feet
   b. 60 feet
   c. 8 feet
   d. 40 feet

4. How many cups are in 3 quarts?
   a. 6 cups
   b. 12 cups
   c. 3 cups
   d. 24 cups

5. There are 30 members in the drama club. The members drank 2 gallons of soda. How many cups of soda were drank?
   a. 32 cups
   b. 16 cups
   c. 48 cups
   d. 320 cups

6. Sarah needs 3 yards of ribbon to finish the Easter decorations. How many inches of ribbon will she need to buy?
   a. 200 inches
   b. 21 inches
   c. 36 inches
   d. 108 inches

7. It took Mike 1 hour to mow one lawn. How long did it take him to mow 4 lawns?
   a. 3 hours
   b. 4 hours
   c. 5 hours
   d. 6 hours

8. Kristen read 15 minutes on Monday, 20 minutes on Tuesday, 10 minutes on Wednesday and 12 minutes on Thursday. What was her total time reading?
   a. 57 minutes
   b. 1 hour
   c. 39 minutes
   d. 2 hours

9. Each meat loaf contains 2 pounds of hamburger. How many ounces are needed for 3?
   a. 96 ounces
   b. 89 ounces
   c. 72 ounces
   d. 24.5 ounces

10. A farm truck weighs 4 tons. How many pounds does the truck weigh?
    a. 8 pounds
    b. 80 pounds
    c. 800 pounds
    d. 8,000 pounds

Copyright © 1999 Contemporary Publishing Company of Raleigh, Inc.

11. How many hours are in two days?
    a. 48 hours
    b. 30 hours
    c. 50 hours
    d. 24 hours

12. How would you weigh this dog?

    a. ounces
    b. pounds
    c. gallons
    d. feet

13. Greg will be in Atlantic City for 5 weeks. How many days will he be there?
    a. 20
    b. 52
    c. 25
    d. 35

14. What part of a day is 12 hours?
    a. $\frac{1}{6}$
    b. $\frac{1}{4}$
    c. $\frac{1}{2}$
    d. $\frac{1}{10}$

15. Jerry is paid every two weeks. How many paychecks does he receive in a 4-week month?
    a. 1
    b. 4
    c. 2
    d. 3

METRIC MEASUREMENTS

Lengths

kilometer - used to measure distance between cities

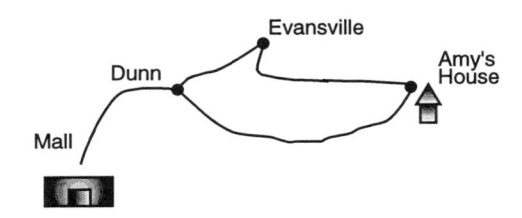

meter - used to measure the length of a cruise ship

centimeter - used to measure the width of a shoe

millimeter - used to measure the thickness of a pencil lead

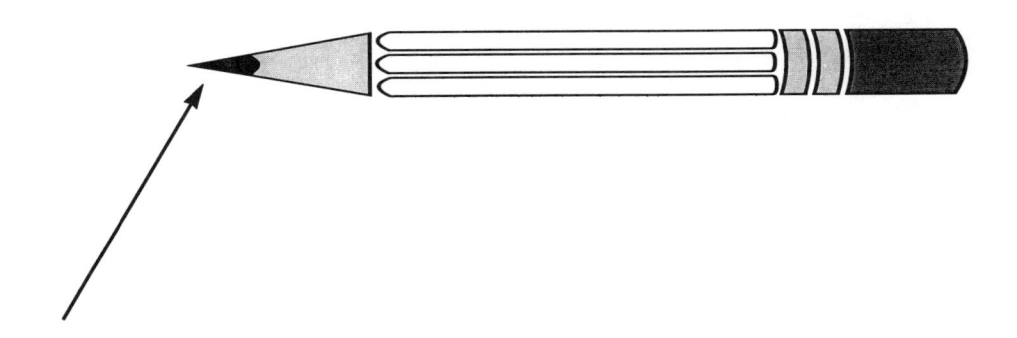

Mass

kilogram - used to measure weight (mass) of a book

gram - used to measure weight (mass) of a pen

milligram - used to measure weight (mass) of a leaf

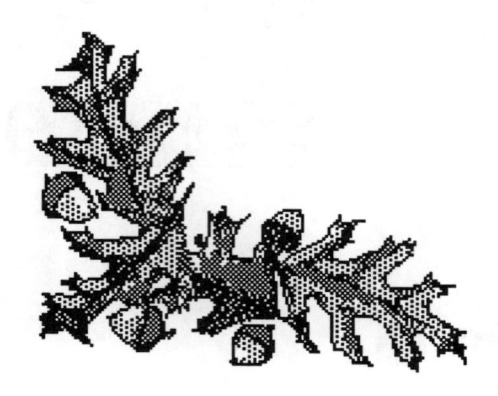

CAPACITY

liter - used to measure the liquid in a tank of gas

milliliter - used to measure the liquid in chemistry equipment

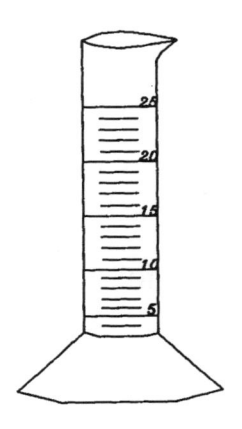

PRACTICE

Choose kilometer, meter, centimeter or millimeter for each of the following.

1. To measure your height, use_____.

2. To measure the length of your fingernail, use_____.

3. To measure the distance from Raleigh to Norfolk, Va., use_____.

4. To measure the width of your shoe, use_____.

Choose kilogram, gram or milligram for each of the following.

5. To measure the mass of a baseball mitt, use_____.

6. To measure a pinch of pepper, use_____.

7. To measure a pencil eraser, use_____.

Choose liter or milliliter for each of the following.

8. To measure the amount of water in a swimming pool, use_____.

9. To measure the amount of milk in an eyedropper, use_____.

Which answer would be the appropriate measurement for each picture?

10. 30 centimeters or 30 meters

11. 100 kilograms or 100 grams

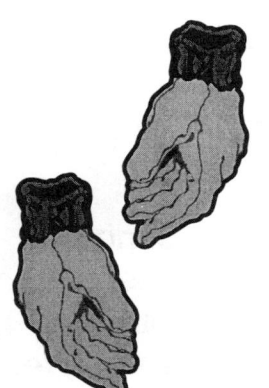

12. 5 grams or 5 milligrams

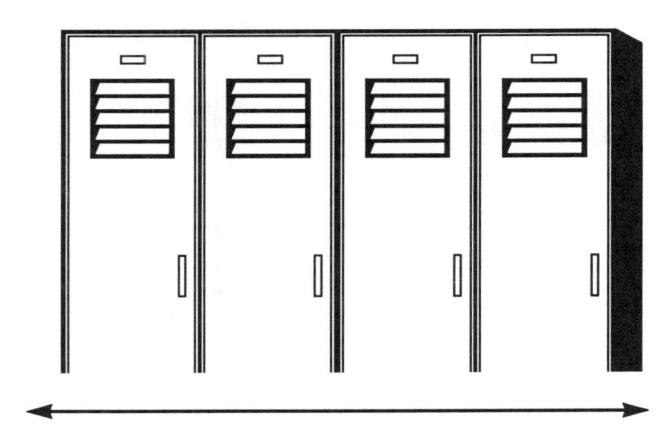

13. 3 kilometers or 3 meters

14. 17 centimeters or 17 kilometers

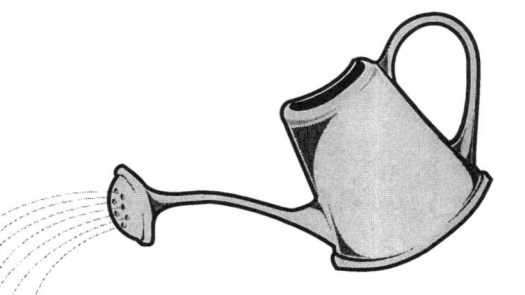

15. 3 liters or 3 milliliters

REVIEW

1. Which would be used to measure the juice in these oranges?

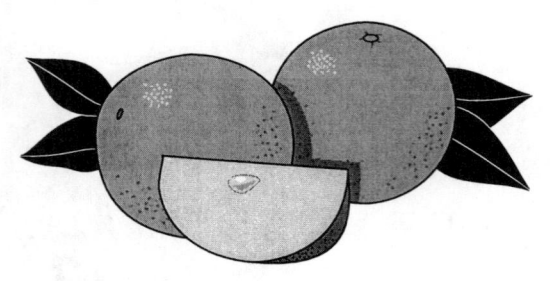

   a. milliliters
   b. meters
   c. liters
   d. centimeters

2. Which would be used to measure these scissors?
   a. meters
   b. grams
   c. centimeters
   d. milligrams

3. Which unit is most appropriate to use when measuring the width of a highway?
   a. millimeter
   b. centimeter
   c. decimeter
   d. meter

4. Which would be used to measure the weight of the Statue of Liberty?

   a. meters
   b. grams
   c. centimeters
   d. kilograms

5. Marjorie's driveway is 30 meters long rounded to the nearest ten. Which of the following could be the length of her driveway before rounding?
   a. 23 meters
   b. 21 meters
   c. 27 meters
   d. 24 meters

6. Which of the following would be measured in kilograms?
   a. pencil
   b. piece of paper (10cm × 12cm)
   c. pin
   d. brick

7. Which of the following would be the appropriate unit to use for measuring a glass of grapefruit juice?
   a. centimeter
   b. gram
   c. liter
   d. milliliter

8. An approximate mass of a leaf would be _____ .
   a. 40 milligrams
   b. 40 grams
   c. 40 kilograms
   d. 40 liters

9. Which would be used to measure the perfume in this bottle? 
   a. gram
   b. milligram
   c. milliliter
   d. centimeter

10. Which would be used to measure the length of this wand? 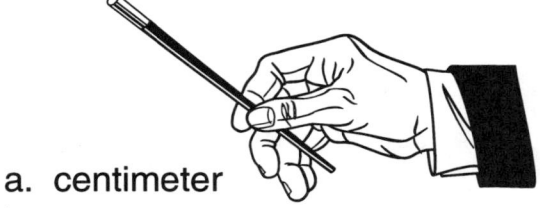
    a. centimeter
    b. gram
    c. milligram
    d. millimeter

11. Which would be used to weigh this bracelet? 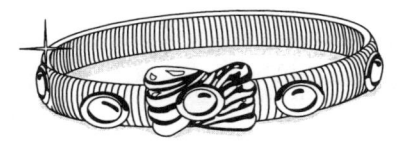
    a. gram
    b. milligram
    c. centimeter
    d. millimeter

12. Which would be used to measure the length of this jet's flight from Raleigh to Chicago? 
    a. meter
    b. kilometer
    c. gram
    d. kilogram

13. Which metric unit would be used to measure the thickness of a hair?
    a. meter
    b. millimeter
    c. centimeter
    d. milligram

14. The approximate weight of a pair of shoes would be _____.
    a. 1 gram
    b. 1 milligram
    c. 1 kilogram
    d. 1 meter

15. The approximate width of a little finger is _____.
    a. 1 meter
    b. 1 kilometer
    c. 1 gram
    d. 1 centimeter

16. Which of the following is not a metric unit of measurement?
    a. gram
    b. quart
    c. liter
    d. centimeter

17. Which would be used to measure this kitten's whiskers?

    a. kilogram
    b. centimeter
    c. millimeter
    d. gram

18. To calculate the mass of a car, use _____.
    a. grams
    b. kilograms
    c. milligrams
    d. milliliters

19. _____ would be used to calculate the capacity of a pot of chili.
    a. milliliters
    b. grams
    c. liters
    d. kilograms

20. The best estimate for a tank of gas would be _____.
    a. 51 kilograms
    b. 51 grams
    c. 51 liters
    d. 51 milliliters

MEASURING TIME

Here is a clock face. The long hand is the **minute** hand. The short hand is the **hour** hand. The time is 5:00.

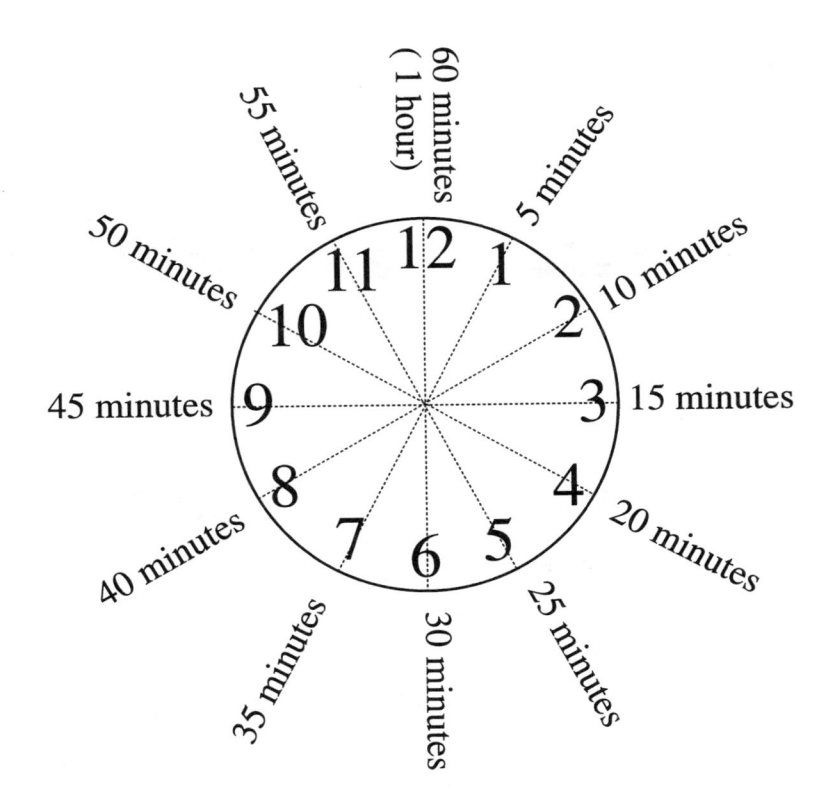

There are 60 minutes in an hour.

89

EXAMPLES

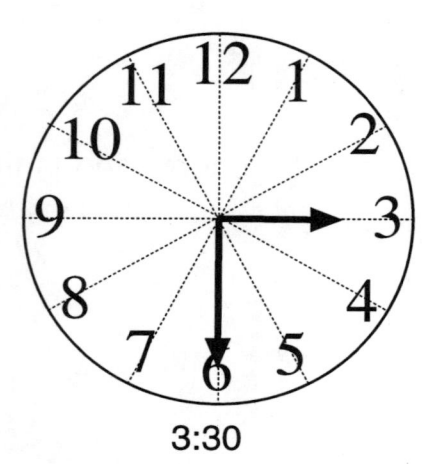

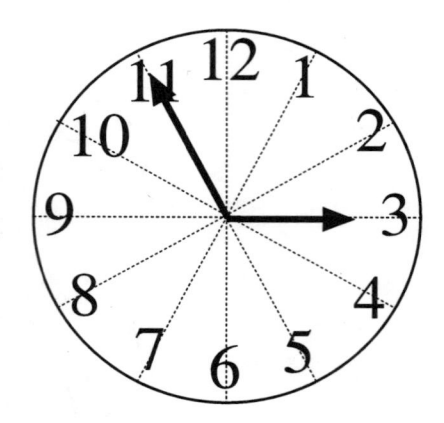

3:00

2:55

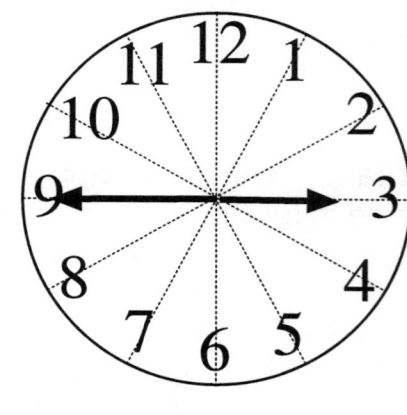

3:30

2:45

WRITING TIME IN OTHER WAYS

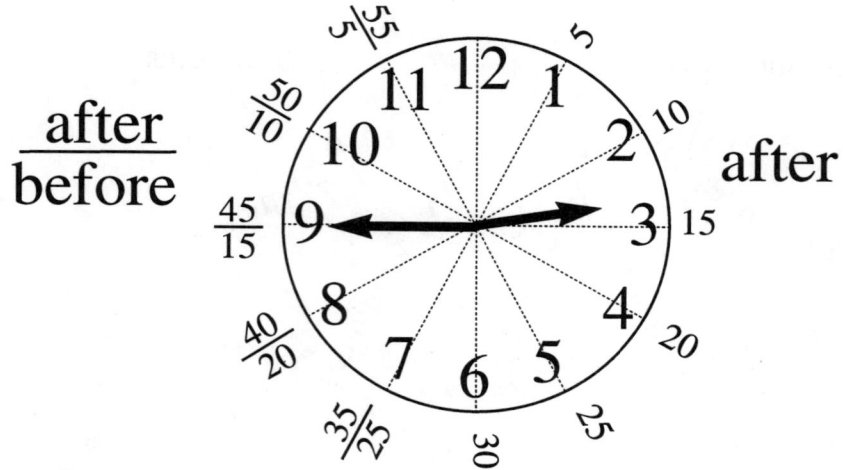

after / before

after

45 minutes after 2:00

15 minutes before 3:00

90

EXAMPLES

3:20   20 minutes after 3:00

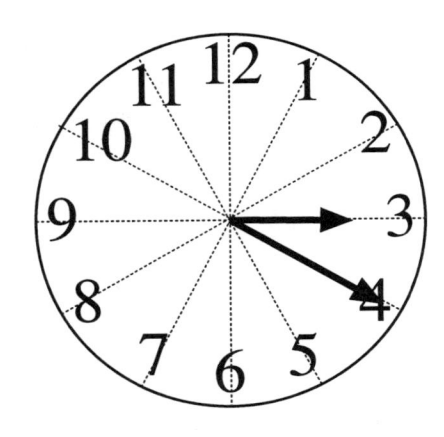

5:40   40 minutes after 5:00
                   20 minutes before 6:00

1:15   15 minutes after 1:00
                   quarter after 1:00

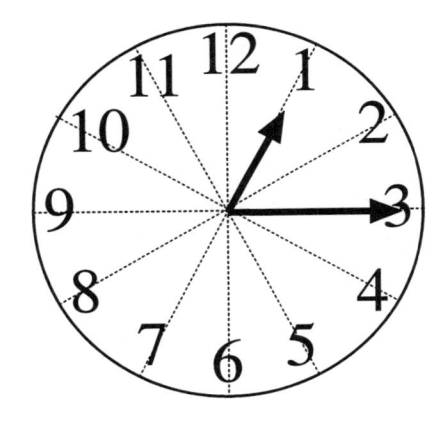

2:45   45 minutes after 2:00
                   15 minutes before 3:00

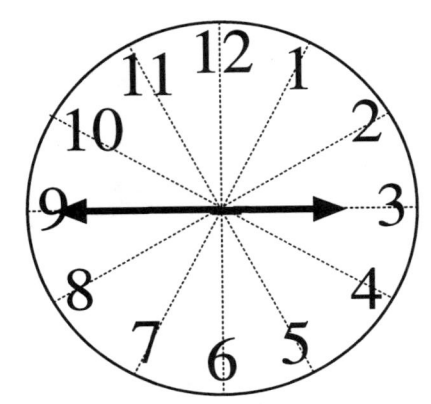

PRACTICE

Draw a clock for each time.

1. 7:30

2. 11:40

3. 1:10

4. 5:00

5. 12:25

6. 8:45

7. 3:05

8. 2:50

9. 7:20

10. 9:00

Write each time in 2 ways.

11. 9:45 _____   _____

12. 3:15 _____   _____

13. 8:50 _____   _____

14. 1:35 _____   _____

15. 5:45 _____   _____

16. 6:55 _____   _____

17. 7:15 _____   _____

18. 2:40 _____   _____

19. 12:15 _____   _____

20. 4:35 _____   _____

REVIEW

1. Cassie has a doctor's appointment at 2:30. Which clock shows the time that Cassie must be at the doctor's office?

   a.

   b.

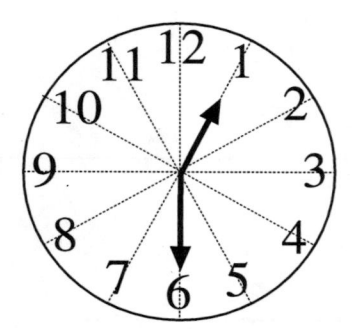

   c.

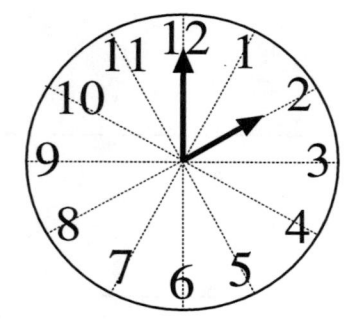

   d.

2. "Quarter after three" is another way of saying which time?
   a. 2:15
   b. 2:45
   c. 3:10
   d. 3:15

3.

   Which clock below has the same time as the one above?

   a. 5:55

   b. 5:10

   c. 4:05

   d. 5:05

4. Which clock shows "10 minutes before 5 o'clock"?

   a.  5:10

   b.  4:50

   c.  4:45

   d.  10:5

5. What time is it?

   a. six minutes before nine
   b. quarter after six
   c. 15 minutes before seven
   d. 15 minutes before six

6. Marlowe must be at piano lessons in 2 hours. If it is 2:00 now, which clock shows the time Marlowe must be at the piano teacher's home for her lesson?

   a.

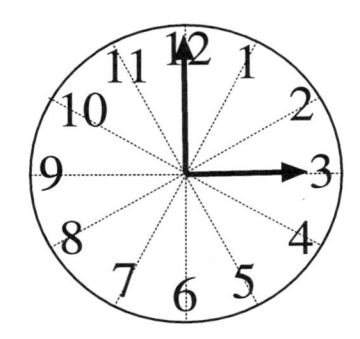

   b.

   c.

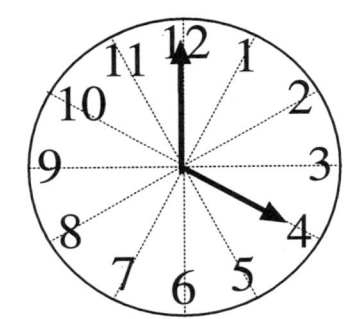

   d.

7. Which clock shows 8:40?
   a.
   b.
   c.
   d.

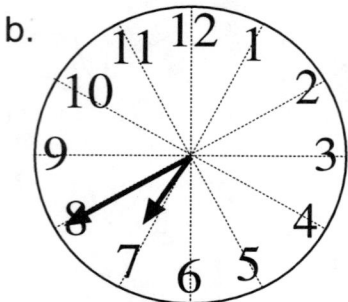

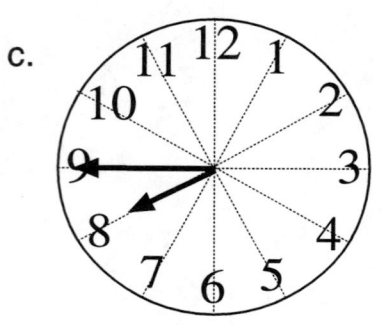

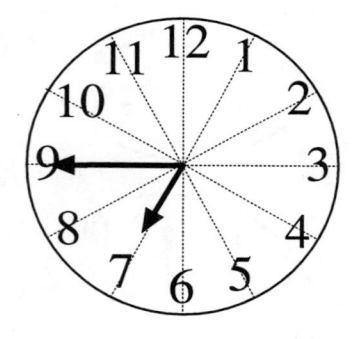

8. Which clock shows "quarter after two"?
   a. 2:45
   b. 2:15
   c. 15:2
   d. 2:30

9. Which of the following is eight o'clock?
   a. 7:50
   b. 8:30
   c. 8:00
   d. 8:15

10. Which of the following shows 9:10?

   a.

   b.

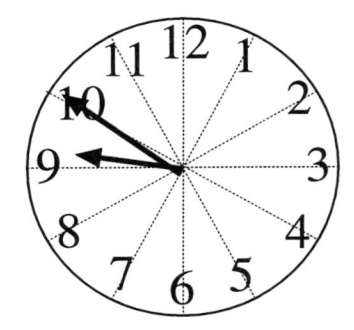

   c.

   d.

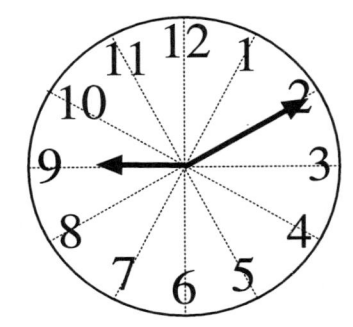

CHAPTER 7

GEOMETRY

ANGLES

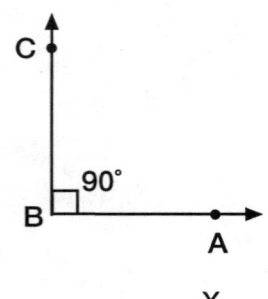

Right Angle – an angle that is exactly 90°

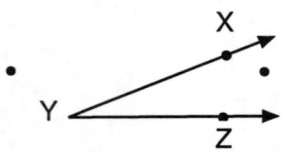

Acute Angle – an angle that is smaller than 90°

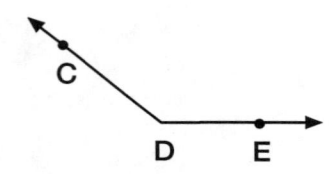

Obtuse Angle – an angle that is larger than 90°

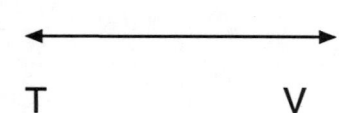

Straight Angle – an angle whose measure is 180°

PRACTICE

Name the kind of angle/angles.

1.

_____

2.

_____

3.

_____

4.

_____

5.

_____

6.

_____

7.

_____

(continued on next page)

8.

_____

9.

_____

10.

_____

11.

_____

12.

_____

Use for #13 and 14.

13. Name 2 acute angles.

_____

_____

14. Name 2 obtuse angles.

_____

_____

POLYGONS

A figure (polygon) that has 4 sides is a quadrilateral. The measures of the angles of a quadrilateral equal 360°.

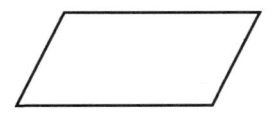

Parallelogram – opposite sides are parallel and equal

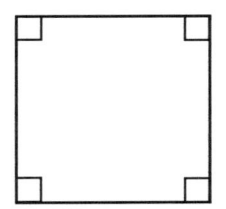

Square – a parallelogram with 4 equal sides and 4 right angles

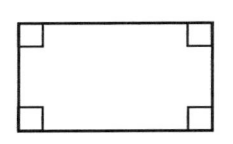

Rectangle – a parallelogram with 4 right angles

OTHER FIGURES

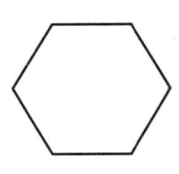

Hexagon – a polygon with 6 sides

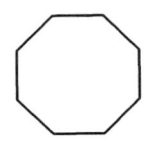

Octagon – a polygon with 8 sides

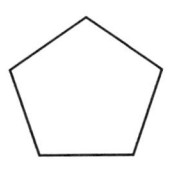

Pentagon – a polygon with 5 sides

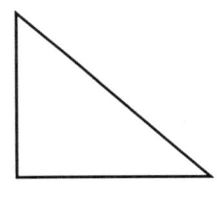

Triangle - a polygon with 3 sides

GEOMETRIC FIGURES — SOLID

Polyhedrons are closed geometric figures that consist of four or more polygons.

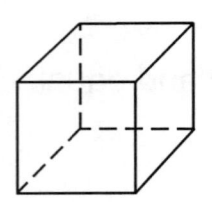

Cube

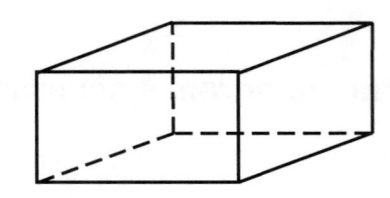

Rectangular prism

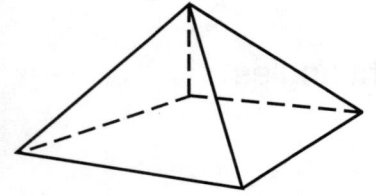

Pyramid

Other solid geometric figures are:

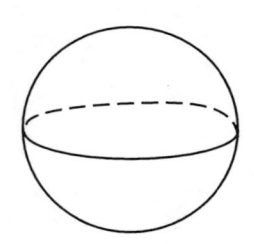

Sphere

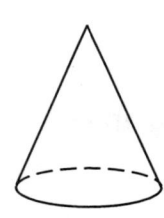

Cone

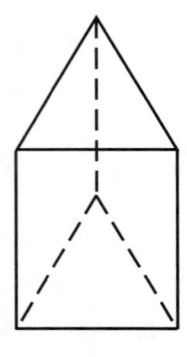

Triangular Prism

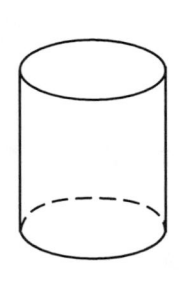

Cylinder

PRACTICE

Name each polygon, polyhedron, or solid geometric figure.

1.

_____

2.

_____

3.

_____

4.

_____

5.

_____

6.

_____

7.

_____

8.

_____

9.

_____

10.

_____

11.

_____

12.

_____

(continued on next page)

13. _____

14. _____

15. _____

16. _____

17. _____

18. _____

Answer each of the following:

19. Which polygons contain right angles? _____

20. Which solid geometric figures contain triangles? _____

21. Which solid geometric figures contain circles? _____

22. Which solid geometric figures contain squares? _____

SIMILAR FIGURES

Figures that are similar look alike except one is larger or smaller than the other.

EXAMPLES

CONGRUENT FIGURES

Figures that are exactly the same are congruent.

EXAMPLES

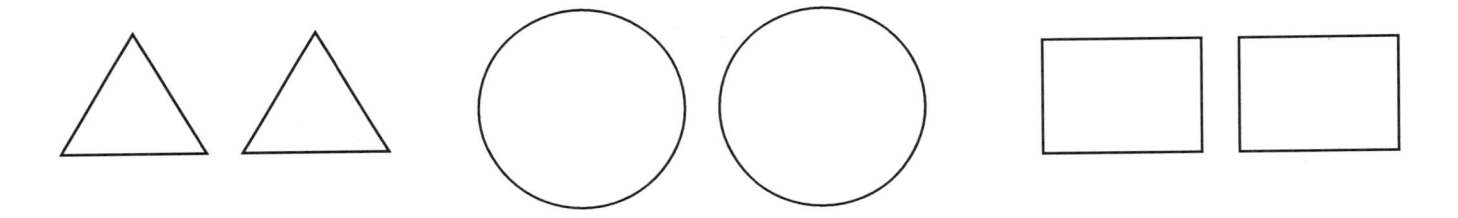

LINES OF SYMMETRY

A line of symmetry divides a figure into 2 identical pieces.

EXAMPLES

Symmetrical   Not Symmetrical

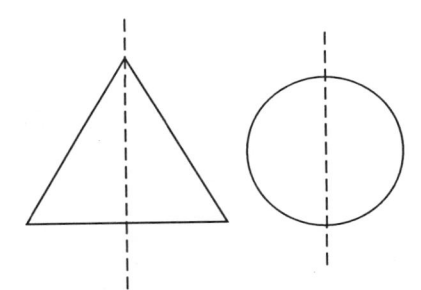

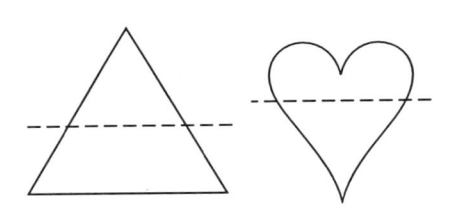

PRACTICE

Draw a figure that is similar to each of the following.

1.

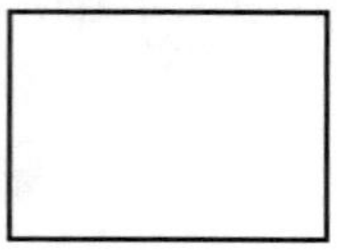

2.

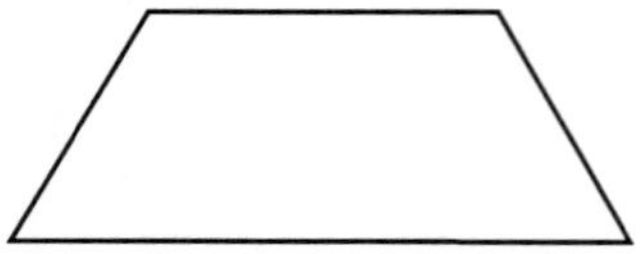

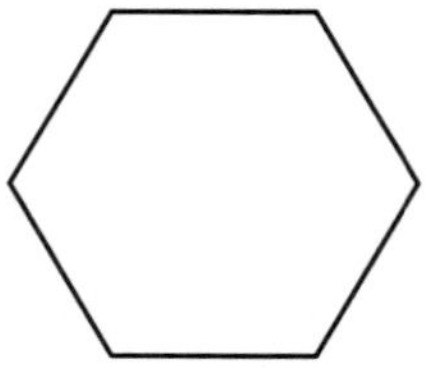

3.

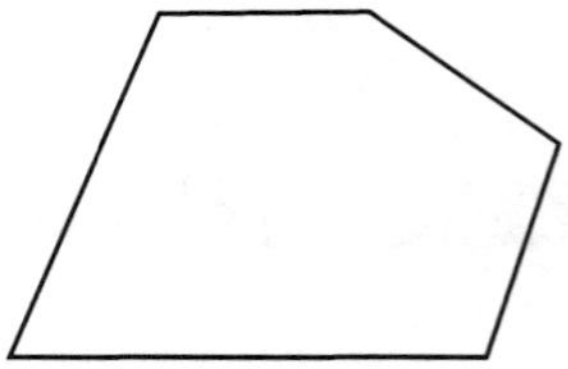

4.

5.

6.

7.

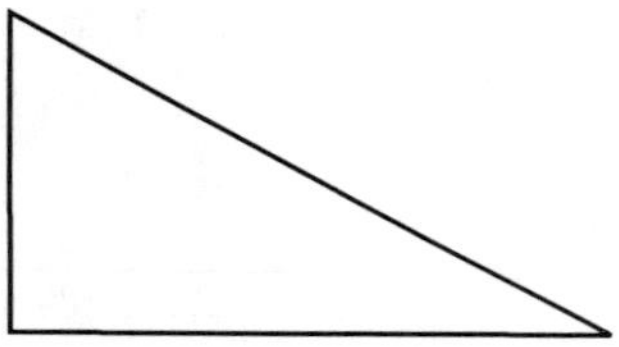

8.

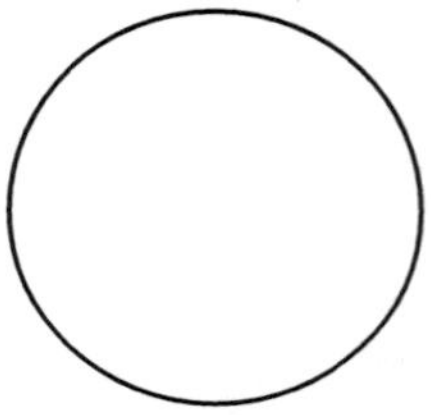

Draw a line of symmetry through each figure.

9.

10.

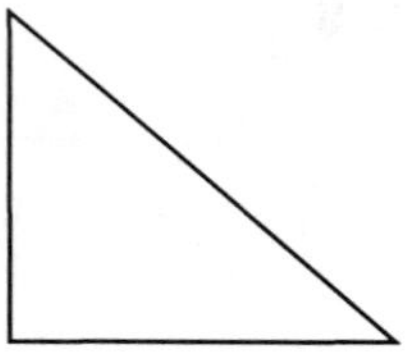

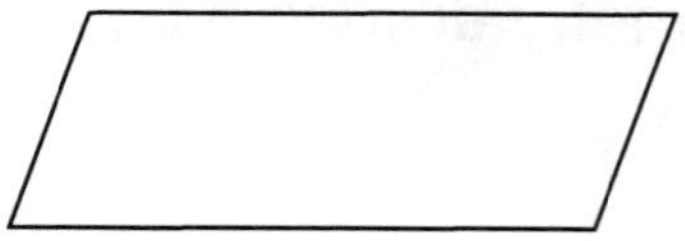

11.

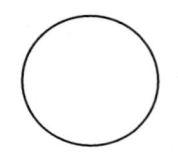

12.

13.

14.

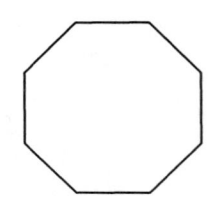

Are these figures congruent? Answer yes or no.

15. _____

16. _____

17. _____

18. _____

19. _____

20. _____

REVIEW

1. A 75° angle is _____.
   a. acute
   b. obtuse
   c. right
   d. straight

2. A 90° angle is _____.
   a. acute
   b. obtuse
   c. right
   d. straight

3. A 165° angle is _____.
   a. acute
   b. obtuse
   c. right
   d. straight

Use this figure to answer questions 4–8.

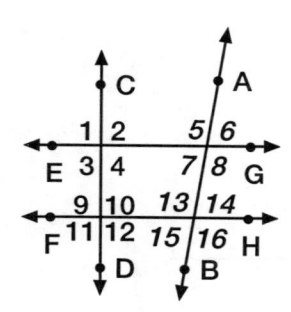

4. Which angle is not a right angle?
   a. ∠1
   b. ∠9
   c. ∠5
   d. ∠12

5. Which 2 angles are obtuse angles?
   a. ∠5, ∠8
   b. ∠10, ∠12
   c. ∠11, ∠12
   d. ∠6, ∠5

6. What pairs are acute angles?
   a. ∠13 and ∠14, ∠15 and ∠16
   b. ∠1 and ∠9, ∠3 and ∠11
   c. ∠2 and ∠5, ∠4 and ∠7
   d. ∠6 and ∠14, ∠7 and ∠15

7. Which angle is obtuse?
   a. ∠6
   b. ∠14
   c. ∠2
   d. ∠5

8. Which 2 angles are right angles?
   a. ∠9, ∠10
   b. ∠7, ∠6
   c. ∠6, ∠5
   d. ∠14, ∠13

9. A quadrilateral has angles whose measurements total ___ degrees.
   a. 30°
   b. 180°
   c. 90°
   d. 360°

10. Which of the following is a straight angle?
    a.
    b.
    c.
    d.

11. A parallelogram with 4 right angles is a _____.
    a. trapezoid
    b. square
    c. rectangle
    d. rhombus

12. A figure with 8 sides is _____.
    a. a square
    b. a pentagon
    c. an octagon
    d. a rectangle

13. [figure] is a _____.
    a. rectangular prism
    b. cube
    c. triangular prism
    d. pyramid

14. Which of the following is a sphere?
    a. [cube]   c. [pyramid]
    b. [sphere] d. [triangular prism]

15. A parallelogram with 4 equal sides and 4 right angles is a _____.
    a. square
    b. rectangle
    c. trapezoid
    d. rhombus

16. A pentagon has ___ sides.
    a. 4
    b. 5
    c. 6
    d. 8

17. Which of the following would be a line of symmetry for this polygon?
    a. b. c. d.

18. A parallelogram has opposite sides that are equal and _____.
    a. parallel
    b. right angles
    c. opposite angles
    d. rhombus

19. Which of the following is similar to [right triangle]?
    a. [parallelogram]
    b. [rectangle]
    c. [triangle]
    d. [right triangle]

20. All of the following are lines of symmetry except which one?
    a. b. c. d.

Copyright © 1999 Contemporary Publishing Company of Raleigh, Inc.

21. Which of the following is the greatest angle?

a.

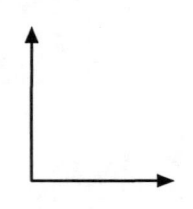

b.

c.

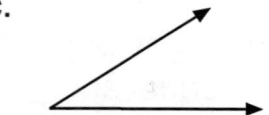

d.

22. Which time represents an acute angle?

a.

b.

c.

d.

110

23. Which of the following figures contains a right angle?
a. 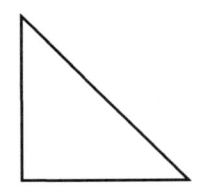
b. 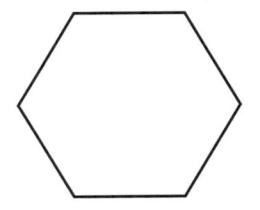
c. 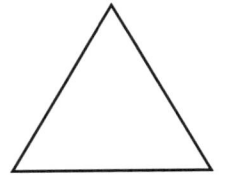
d.

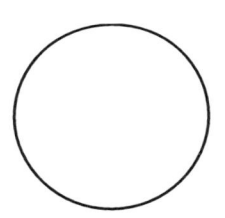

24. Which of the following best describes this picture?
a. a cone
b. a pyramid
c. a square
d. a triangle

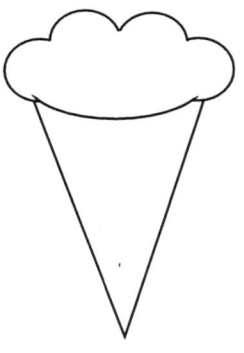

25. Which of the following is not a polygon?
a. 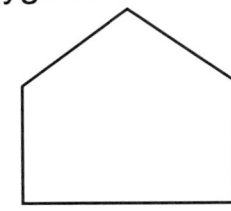
b. 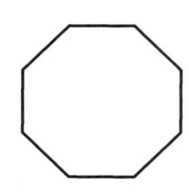
c. 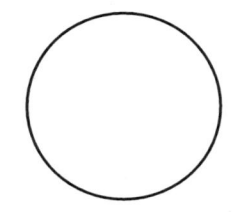
d.

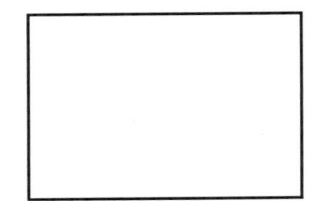

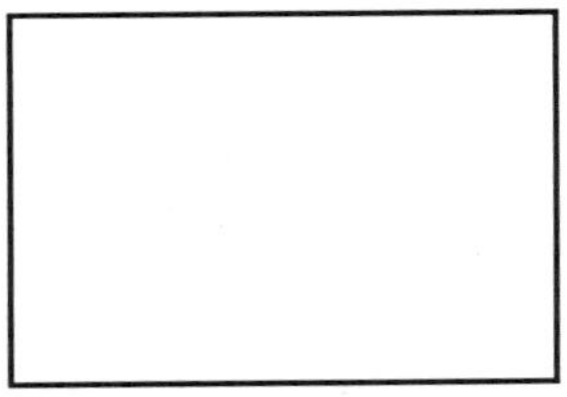

26. Which of the following chould be traced to draw a square?
a. 
b. 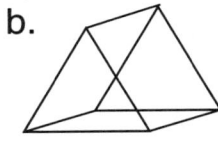
c. 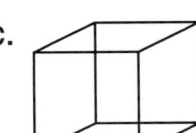
d.

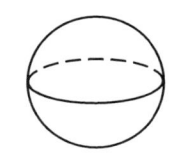

27. Which group of figures is congruent?
    a.
    b.
    c.
    d.

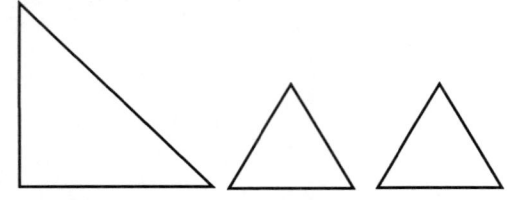

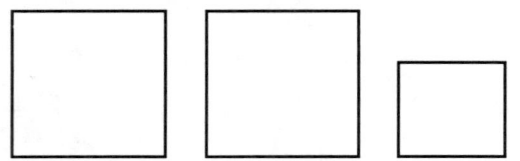

28. Which figure below is congruent to the figure in the circle?

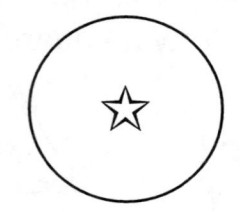

    a.
    b.
    c.
    d.

29. Which of the following contains at least one triangle?
    a. cone
    b. square
    c. sphere
    d. pyramid

30. Which of the following is a rectangular prism?
    a. a basketball
    b. a box
    c. a pencil point
    d. a tack

CHAPTER 8

AREA

Area is the region inside a figure.

AREA FORMULAS AND EXAMPLES

Square A = s × s (side × side)

A = 10 × 10
A = 100

(square with side 10)

Rectangle A = l × w (length × width)

A = 9 × 6
A = 54

(rectangle 9 by 6)

Copyright © 1999 Contemporary Publishing Company of Raleigh, Inc.

113

PRACTICE

Find the area of each.

1. Rectangle: l = 4 w = 8

2. Square: s = 5

3. Square: s = 3

4. Rectangle: l = 8 w = 7

5. Rectangle: w = 8 l = 9

6. Rectangle: l = 8 w = 4

7. Square: s = 7

8. Square: s = 10

9. Rectangle: l = 3 w = 11

10. Rectangle: l = 12 w = 9

11. Rectangle: l = 7 w = 10

12. Square: s = 9

13. Rectangle: l = 5 w = 9

14. ▢ 8

15.

   7
┌──────────┐
│   │ 5
└──────────┘

18.

    8
┌────────┐
│   │ 6
└────────┘

16.

  6
┌────┐
│   │
└────┘

19.

  2
┌────┐
│   │
└────┘

17.

    4
┌────────┐
│   │
│   │
└────────┘

20.

     11
┌──────────┐
│   │ 2
└──────────┘

REVIEW

1. What is the area of the shaded section?
   a. 42
   b. 10
   c. 12
   d. 30

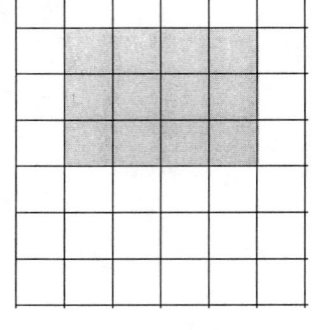

2. Tom wants to fertilize his front yard. The yard is 10 feet square. What is the total area to be fertilized?
   a. 20 square feet
   b. 40 square feet
   c. 100 square feet
   d. 10 square feet

3. A photograph measures 10" by 7". What is the area of the photograph?
   a. 70 square inches
   b. 17 square inches
   c. 34 square inches
   d. 3 square inches

4. Which number sentence should be used to find the area of this rectangle? 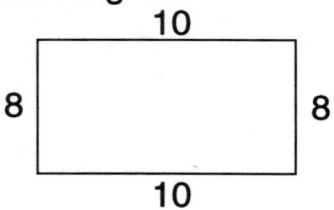
   a. (10 × 8) + (10 × 8)
   b. (2 × 8) + (2 × 10)
   c. 10 × 8
   d. (10 + 8) + (10 + 8)

5. What is the area of this figure? 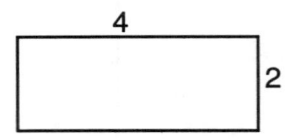
   a. 12
   b. 8
   c. 6
   d. 42

6. What is the area of this figure? 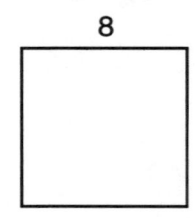
   a. 16
   b. 64
   c. 32
   d. 24

7. How many square feet are in this room? 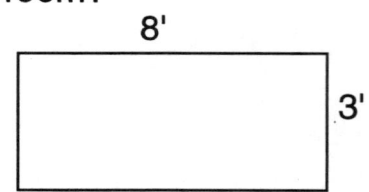
   a. 22 sq. ft.
   b. 21 sq. ft.
   c. 24 sq. ft.
   d. 32 sq. ft.

8. A rectangle has a width of 8 and a height of 10. What is its area?
   a. 36
   b. 80
   c. 18
   d. 30

9. If the length of a rectangle is 6 and the width is 8, what is the area?
   a. 28
   b. 14
   c. 56
   d. 48

10. Marshall's garden is 9 feet long and 7 feet wide. How many square feet does the garden cover?
    a. 32 square feet
    b. 63 square feet
    c. 16 square feet
    d. 66 square feet

11. Which of the following best describes the area of the rectangle as compared to the area of the square?

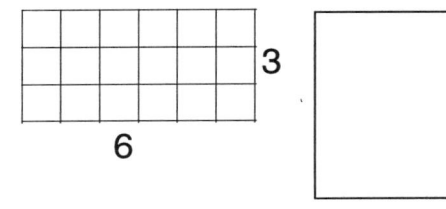

    a. The area of the rectangle is larger.
    b. The area of the square is smaller.
    c. The area of the square is larger.
    d. The areas are the same.

Use the figure to answer questions 12–15.

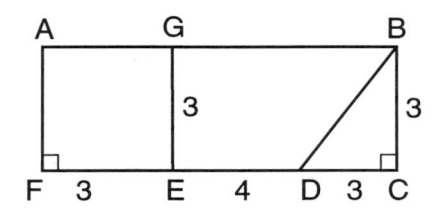

12. What formula would you use to find the area of figure ABCF?
    a. $A = s \times s$
    b. $A = 2 \times s$
    c. $A = 2 \times l \times w$
    d. $A = lw$

13. What formula would you use to find the area of figure AFEG?
    a. $A = s \times s$
    b. $A = lw$
    c. $A = 2 \times s$
    d. $A = 2 \times l \times w$

14. What is the area of figure ABCF?
    a. 28
    b. 20
    c. 30
    d. 14

15. What is the area of figure AFEG?
    a. 12
    b. 9
    c. 3
    d. 6

16. What is the area of this figure?

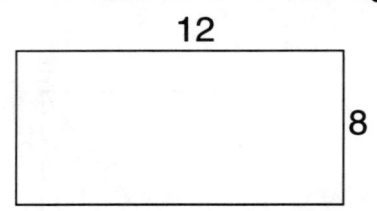

12
8

a. 20
b. 40
c. 30
d. 96

17. What is the area?

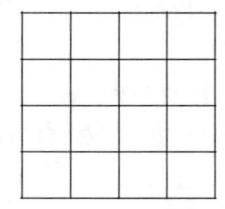

a. 8
b. 16
c. 4
d. 20

18. What is the area?

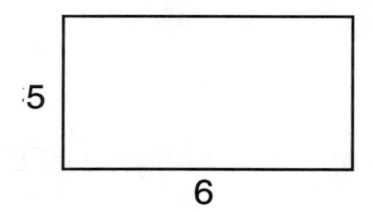

5
6

a. 36
b. 11
c. 30
d. 22

19. What is the area?

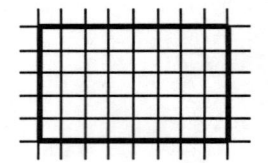

a. 16
b. 48
c. 40
d. 28

20. What is the area?

2

a. 9
b. 10
c. 8
d. 4

21. What is the area of this square?

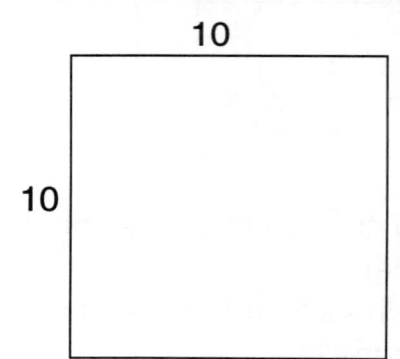

10
10

a. 40
b. 100
c. 20
d. 90

22. How many square-inch pieces are in this 1 foot square puzzle?

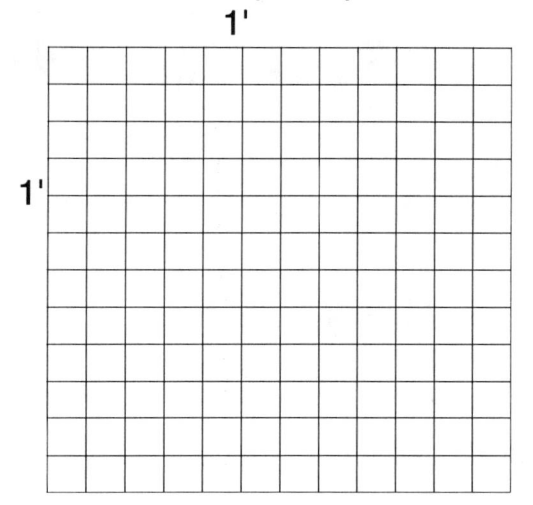

1'

1'

a. 1,100
b. 10
c. 1
d. 100

23. What is the area?

9

4

a. 13
b. 36
c. 26
d. 40

24. What is the area of a square with a side of 1?
a. 11
b. 2
c. 4
d. 1

25. What formula did you use to solve #24?
a. $A = 2 \times s$
b. $A = s \times s$
c. $A = lw$
d. $A = 2 \times l \times w$

CHAPTER 9

PERIMETER

Perimeter is the distance around a polygon (triangle, square, rectangle, etc.). You add **all** the lengths of the sides to find the perimeter.

EXAMPLES

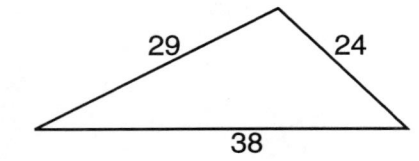

Perimeter (Triangle):
29 + 24 + 38 = 91
(3 sides)

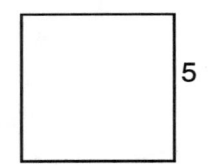

Perimeter (Square):
5 + 5 + 5 + 5 = 20
(4 sides)

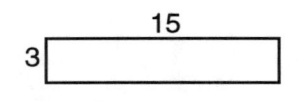

Perimeter (Rectangle):
15 + 15 + 3 + 3 = 36
(4 sides)

PRACTICE

Find the perimeter of each square.

1. side = 39

2. side = 18

3. side = 3

4. side = 9

Find the perimeter of each rectangle.

5. l = 5 w = 3

6. l = 37 w = 12

7. l = 15 w = 13

8. l = 813 w = 764

Find the perimeter of each triangle.

9. sides = 14, 7, 21

10. sides = 35, 23, 94

11. sides = 2, 1, 3

12. sides = 121, 136, 100

13. A triangular tablecloth has sides of 25", 25", 25". How much binding would you need to go around this tablecloth?

14. Don put a fence around his flower garden. The garden is 30' by 20'. How many feet of fence did he need to buy to go around the garden?

15. Marilyn made a baby blanket 3' by 3'. How much ribbon was needed to go around the outside edge?

16. A wooden rail was put around the parking lot of the supermarket. The lot is 15' × 10'. How many feet of rail must be bought to go around the parking lot?

REVIEW

1. Find the perimeter.

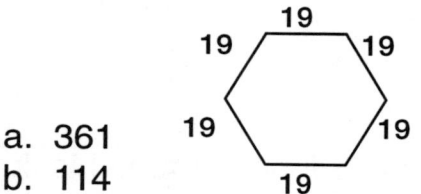

   a. 361
   b. 114
   c. 152
   d. 224

2. Find the perimeter.

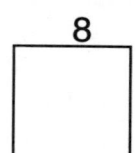

   a. 64
   b. 8
   c. 16
   d. 32

3. Find the perimeter.

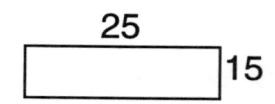

   a. 80
   b. 40
   c. 55
   d. 375

4. Find the perimeter.

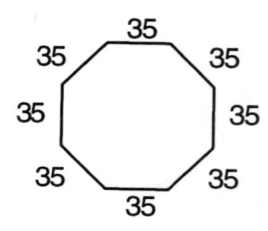

   a. 21
   b. 1,225
   c. 28
   d. 245

5. Find the perimeter.

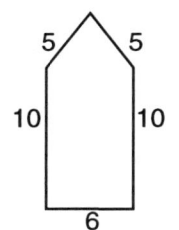

   a. 50
   b. 56
   c. 131
   d. 36

6. Find the perimeter.

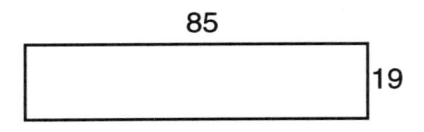

   a. 104
   b. 208
   c. 807.5
   d. 1,615

7. What is the perimeter of a square with a side of 40?
   a. 160
   b. 80
   c. 1,600
   d. 120

8. A rectangle has a length of 53 in. and a width of 38 in. What is the perimeter?
   a. 2,014 in.
   b. 91 in.
   c. 182 in.
   d. 201.4 in.

9. What expression would you use to find the perimeter of a triangle with sides of 25, 29, and 14?
   a. 25 × 29 + 14
   b. 25 + 29 × 14
   c. 25 × 29 × 14
   d. 25 + 29 + 14

10. The perimeter of this square is 16. How did you find the perimeter?

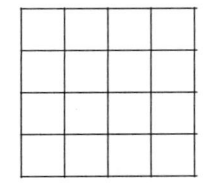

    a. length × width
    b. ½ length + width
    c. 4 times length of a side
    d. 3 times length of a side

11. A picture of John's niece is a square with sides of 126 inches. What is the perimeter of the picture?
    a. 252 in.
    b. 504 in.
    c. 15,876 in.
    d. 252 in.

12. Which polygon's perimeter is not the same as a square with a side of 4?
   a. 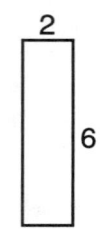 rectangle 2 by 6
   b. 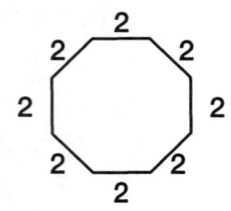 octagon with sides of 2
   c. 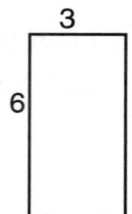 rectangle 3 by 6
   d. 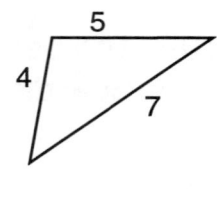 triangle with sides 5, 4, 7

13. Kart Lake has three sides with lengths of 5 1/7 mi., 4 3/7 mi., and 2 1/7 mi. What is the perimeter?
   a. 11 2/7 mi.
   b. 11 8/14 mi.
   c. 11 5/21 mi.
   d. 11 5/7 mi.

14. Which of the following could be the perimeter of a rectangle with an area of 54 square yards?
   a. 27 yd.
   b. 9 yd.
   c. 6 yd.
   d. 30 yd.

15. What is the perimeter of a field with 4 sides of 35 km?
   a. 1,225 km
   b. 140 km
   c. 7 km
   d. 105 km

16. A kitchen is 14 ft. by 18 ft. How much molding would be needed to go around the bottom of the 4 walls?
   a. 64 ft.
   b. 252 ft.
   c. 32 ft.
   d. 16 ft.

17. What is the perimeter? 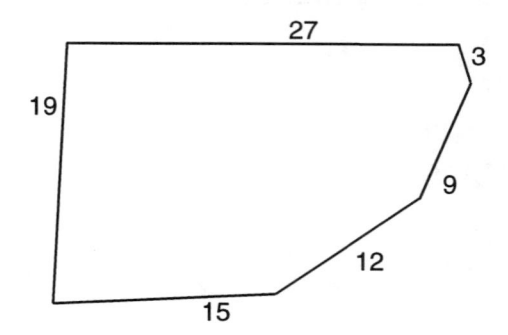
   a. 170
   b. 85
   c. 42.5
   d. 65

18. What expression would you use to find the perimeter of a rectangle 15 in. by 8 in.?
   a. 15 + 15 + 8
   b. 15 + 8 + 8
   c. 15 + 15 + 8 + 8
   d. 15 × 8

19. An octagon has 8 equal sides. If a side is 79, what is the perimeter?
   a. 32
   b. 1,264
   c. 64
   d. 632

20. What is the difference between the perimeters of a square with a side of 10 in. and a triangle with a side of 10 in.?
   a. 0 in.
   b. 1,200 in.
   c. 10 in.
   d. 100 in.

21. A rectangular garden measures 75 yds. by 92 yds. How many yards of wire must you use to put a fence around this garden?
   a. 668 yds.
   b. 334 yds.
   c. 167 yds.
   d. 835 yds.

22. What is the perimeter?

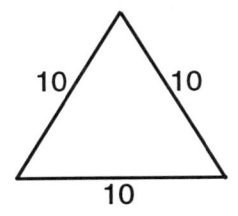

   a. 30
   b. 100
   c. 20
   d. 40

10 CHAPTER

VOLUME

THREE-DIMENSIONAL FIGURES

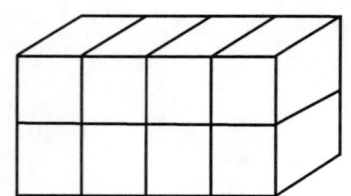

Three-dimensional figures have 3 different views (ways of being seen).

side (end) view

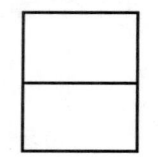

front or back view

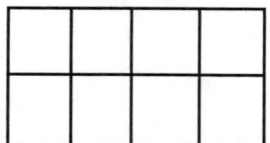

top or bottom view

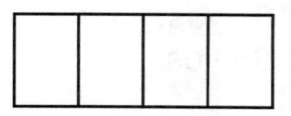

PRACTICE

Draw the side (end) view, front/back view, and top/bottom view of each 3-dimensional figure.

1.

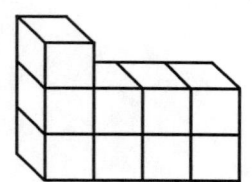

2.

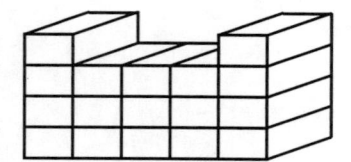

3.

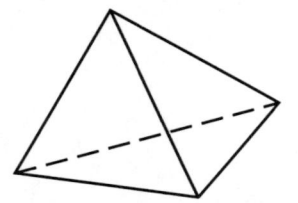

126

Copyright © 1999 Contemporary Publishing Company of Raleigh, Inc.

Draw the top view of the following figures.

4.

5.

6.

7.

FACES, EDGES, AND VERTICES

Faces of a 3-dimensional figure are the polygons and their interiors.

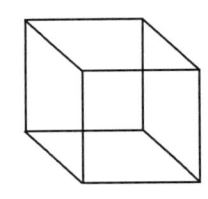

EXAMPLE   A cube has 6 square faces.

Edges of a 3 dimensional figure are line segments where the faces intersect.

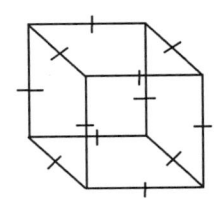

EXAMPLE   A cube has 12 edges.

Vertices of a 3-dimensional figure are points where the edges intersect.

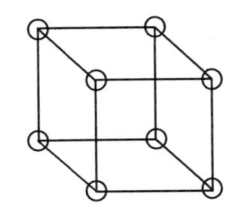

EXAMPLE   A cube has 8 vertices.

Copyright © 1999 Contemporary Publishing Company of Raleigh, Inc.

MAKING FIGURES

EXAMPLE

What 3-dimensional figure will the 2-dimensional pattern make when folded?

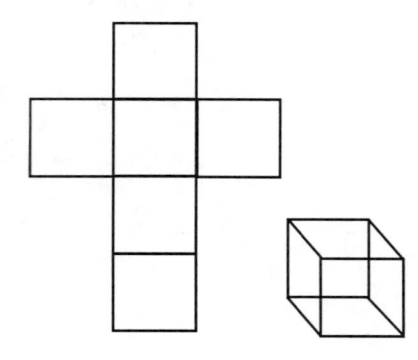

A cube.

PRACTICE

Draw the 3-dimensional figure that will be made when the 2-dimensional pattern is folded.

1.

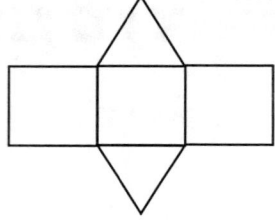

2.

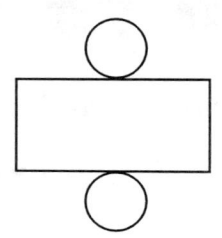

3.

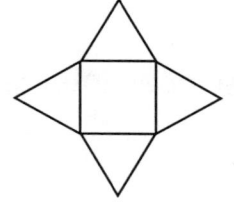

4.

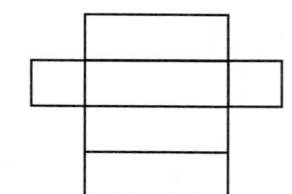

5.

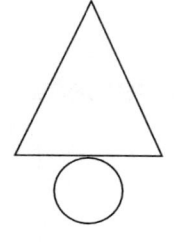

128

Copyright © 1999 Contemporary Publishing Company of Raleigh, Inc.

How many faces, vertices, and edges are in each figure?

6. Rectangular Solid

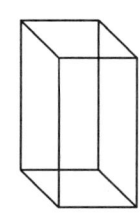

faces _____
vertices _____
edges _____

7. Pyramid

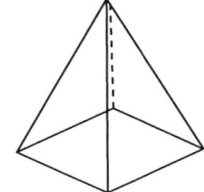

faces _____
vertices _____
edges _____

8. Triangular Prism

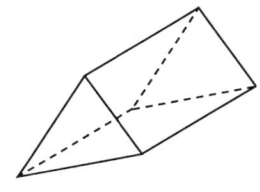

faces _____
vertices _____
edges _____

9. Triangular Prism

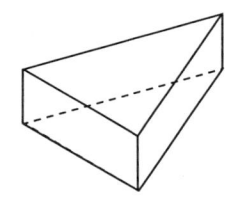

faces _____
vertices _____
edges _____

10. Cube

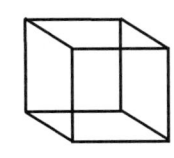

faces _____
vertices _____
edges _____

11. Hexagonal Prism

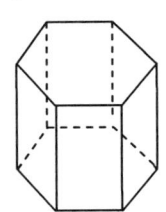

faces _____
vertices _____
edges _____

VOLUME

Volume is how much something can hold.

EXAMPLES

How many cubes were used to build this figure?

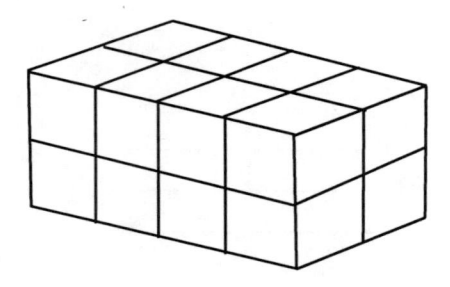

There are 2 layers of 8 cubes so there are 16 cubes.

Draw a figure with a volume of 4 cubes.

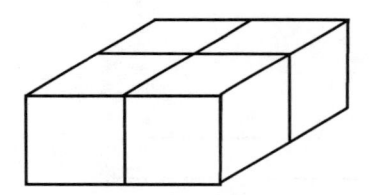

PRACTICE

Draw a figure for each volume.

1. 9 cubes

2. 6 cubes

3. 8 cubes

4. 10 cubes

5. 12 cubes

6. 3 cubes

7. 2 cubes

8. 14 cubes

9. 15 cubes

10. 18 cubes

(continued on next page)

Find the volume of each figure.

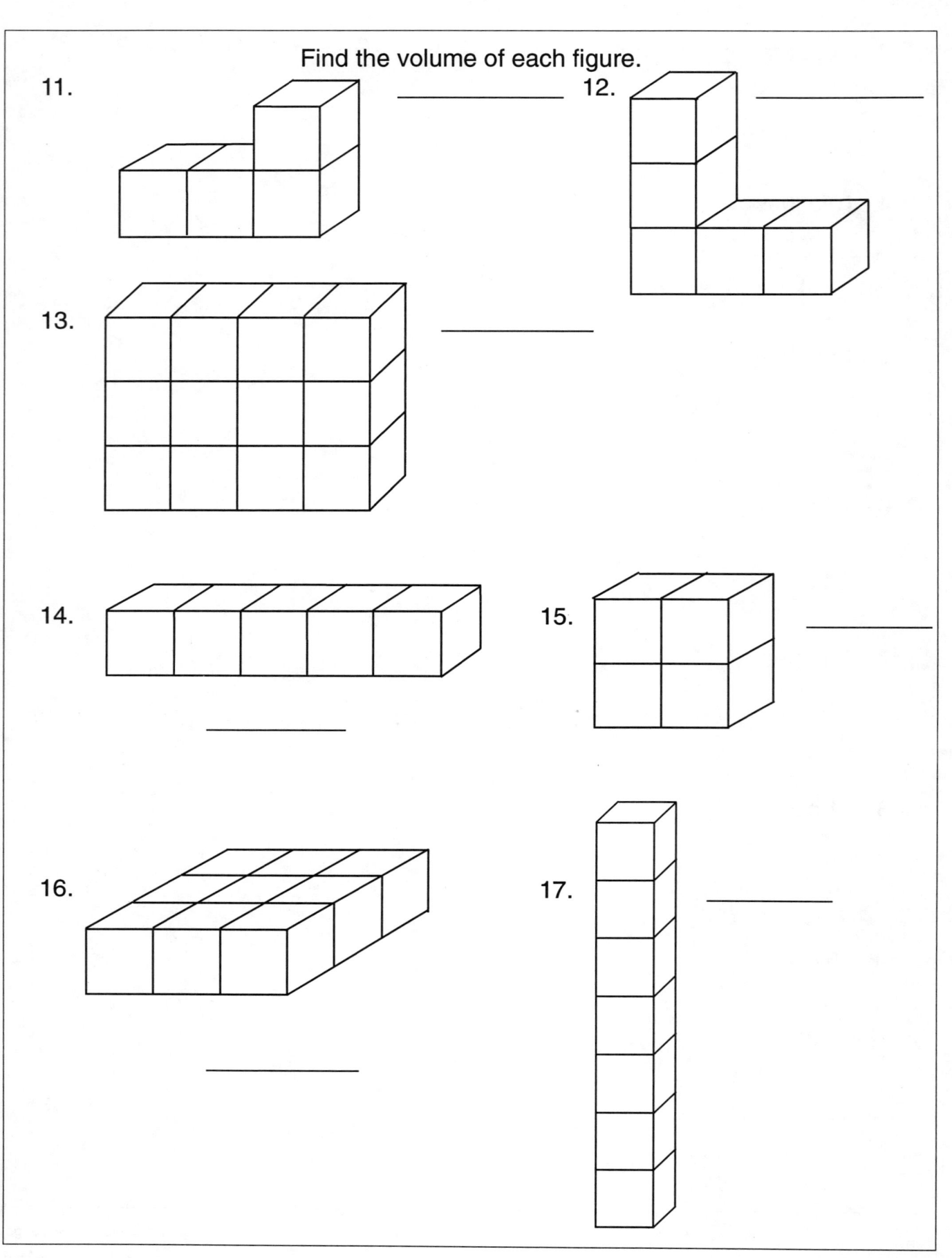

11. _____

12. _____

13. _____

14. _____

15. _____

16. _____

17. _____

REVIEW

1. What is the top view of this figure?

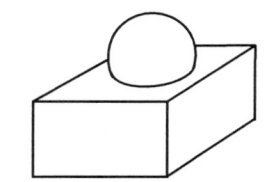

   a. 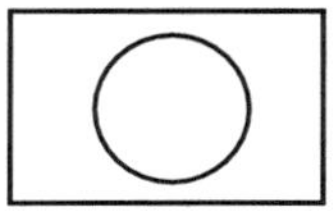
   b. 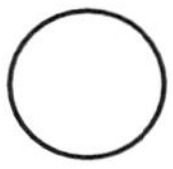
   c. 
   d.

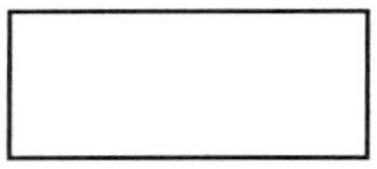

2. What is the bottom view of the figure in question #1?

   a. 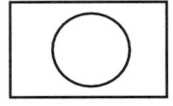
   b. 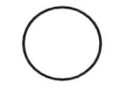
   c. 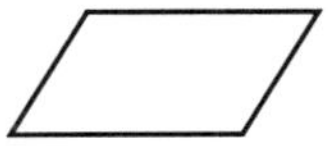
   d.

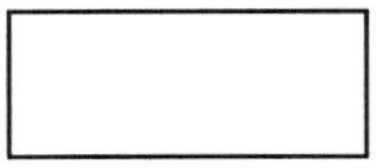

3. What is the side view of this figure?

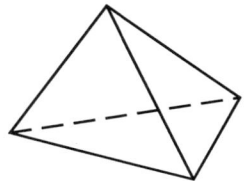

   a. 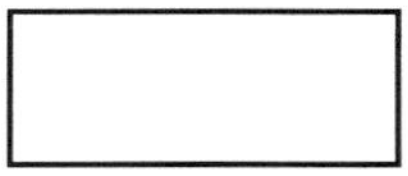
   b. 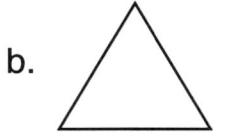
   c. 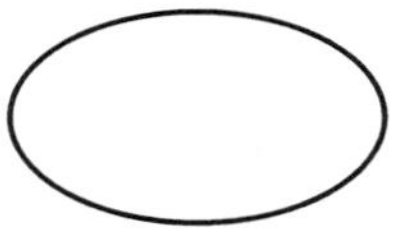
   d.

4. What is the side (end) view of this figure?

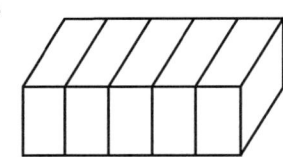

   a. 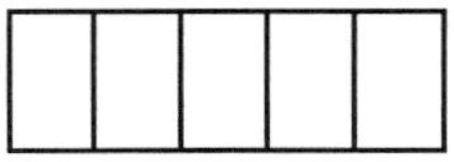
   b. 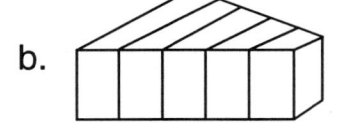
   c. 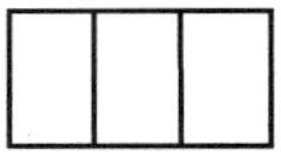
   d.

5. What is the bottom view of the figure in question 4?

   a. 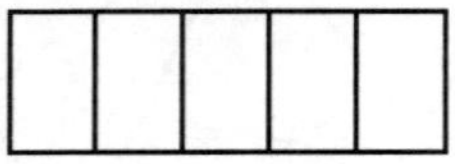 ▭▭▭▭▭ (row of rectangles)

   b. 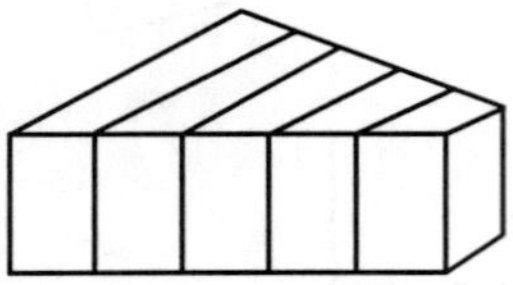 (prism shape)

   c. 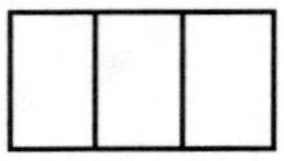 ▭▭▭ (three rectangles)

   d. ▭

6. What is the bottom view of this figure?

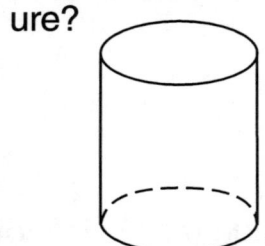

   (cylinder)

   a. 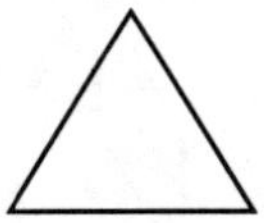 △

   b. ▢

   c. 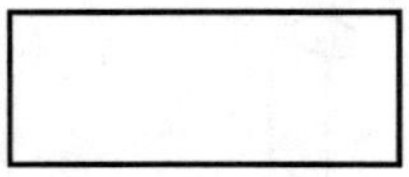 ▭

   d. 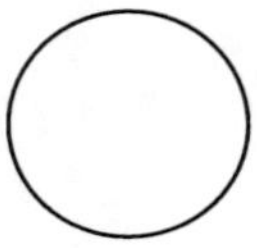 ○

7. What is the side view of this cube?

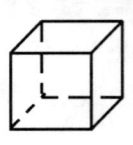

   (cube)

   a. 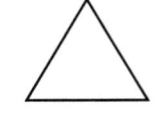 △

   b. ▢

   c.  ○

   d. 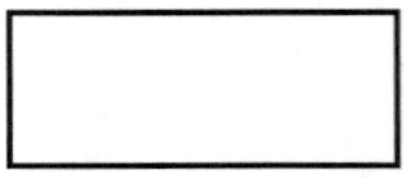 ▭

8. What is the top view of the figure in #7?

   a. 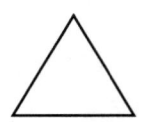 △

   b. 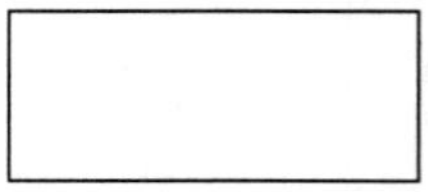 ▭

   c. 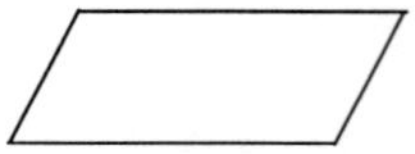 ▱

   d. ▢

134

9. How many edges and vertices does this figure have?

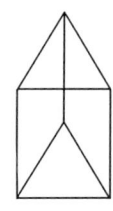

   a. 9 edges and 6 vertices
   b. 5 edges and 8 vertices
   c. 10 edges and 10 vertices
   d. 6 vertices and 9 edges

10. Which of the following statements is true about this figure?

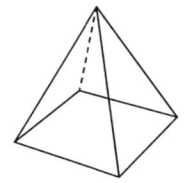

    a. This pyramid has 8 faces and 5 edges.
    b. This pyramid has 6 faces and 10 edges.
    c. This pyramid has 4 faces and 0 edges.
    d. This pyramid has 5 faces and 8 edges.

11. How many faces does this figure have?

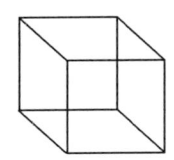

    a. 4 faces
    b. 8 faces
    c. 6 faces
    d. 7 faces

12. What is the 3-dimensional figure shown below?
    top view   bottom view

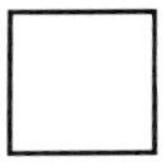

    a. cube
    b. pyramid
    c. cone
    d. cylinder

13. What 3-dimensional figure would be made when you fold this 2-dimensional figure?

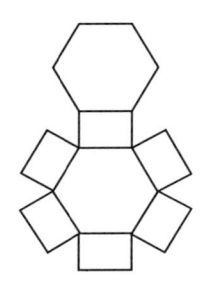

    a. 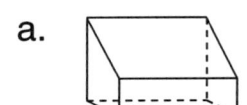
    b. 
    c. 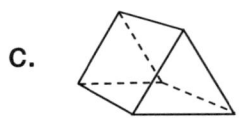
    d.

Copyright © 1999 Contemporary Publishing Company of Raleigh, Inc.

14. What 3-dimensional figure would be made when you fold this 2-dimensional figure?

    a. cylinder
    b. pyramid
    c. cone
    d. cube

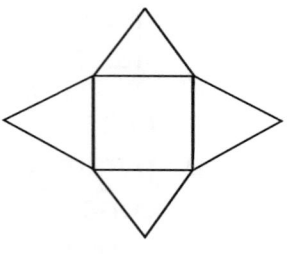

15. Which figure has a circle as its base?
    a. cube
    b. pyramid
    c. cone
    d. triangle

16. Which 2-dimensional figure represents [box] when it is unfolded?

    a.
    b.
    c.
    d.

17. What figure can have a square as its base?
    a. cone
    b. pyramid
    c. cylinder
    d. sphere

18. Marlowe is painting the dots on a block to represent a die. On how many faces must she paint dots?
    a. 4
    b. 8
    c. 6
    d. 9

19. What shapes make up the faces of this 3-dimensional figure?

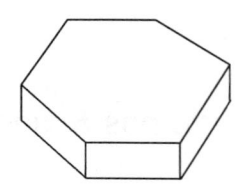

    a. 2 pentagons and 6 squares
    b. 6 squares and 2 triangles
    c. 2 hexagons and 6 rectangles
    d. 2 triangles and 6 rectangles

20. Which of the following has the greatest volume?
    a. 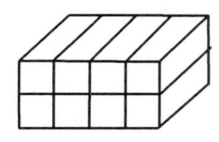
    b. 
    c. 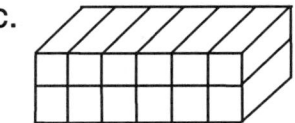
    d.

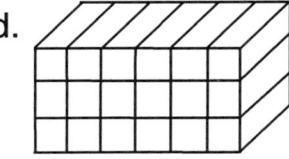

21. What is the volume of this block?

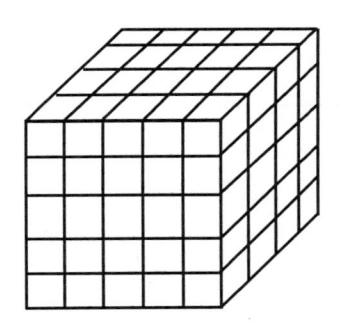

    a. 100
    b. 20
    c. 140
    d. 120

22. This cube is marked for volume. What is the model's volume?

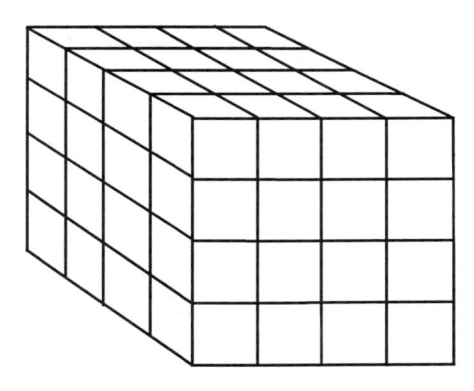

    a. 64
    b. 16
    c. 12
    d. 512

23. If each block has a volume of 1cm.^{3}, what is the volume of this figure?

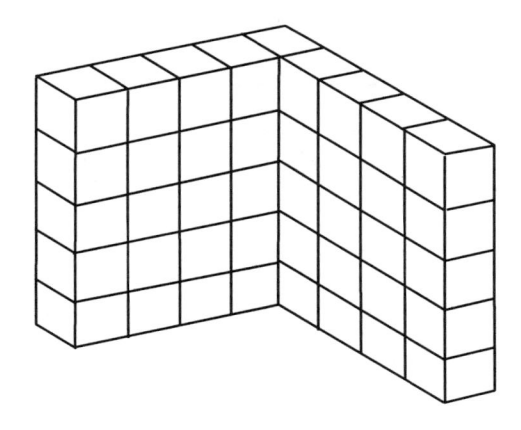

    a. 50 cm.^{3}
    b. 32 cm.^{3}
    c. 45 cm.^{3}
    d. 49 cm.^{3}

24. How many cubes were used to build this figure?

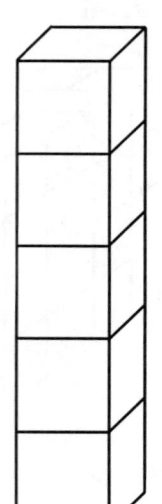

   a. 4
   b. 10
   c. 5
   d. 6

25. Which figure has the smallest volume?
   a. 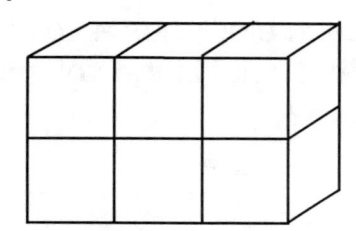
   b. 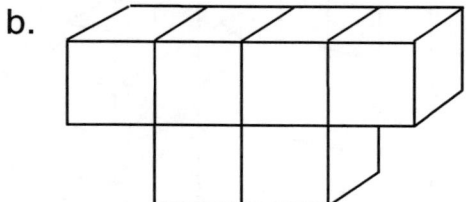
   c. 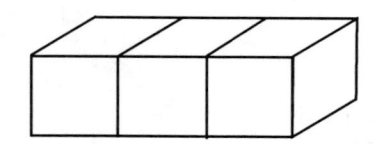
   d.

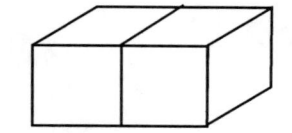

26. How many cubes were used to build this figure?

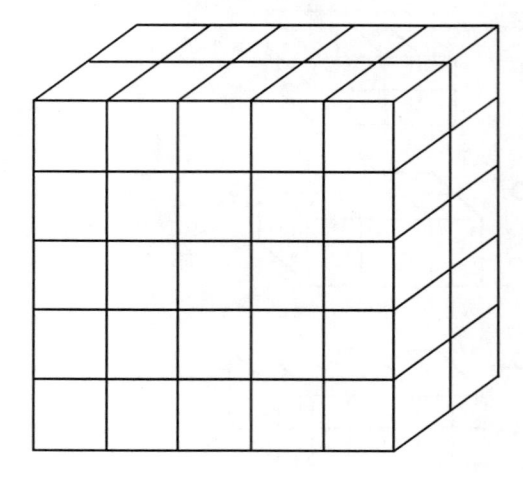

   a. 25
   b. 50
   c. 20
   d. 65

27. If Abigail has 10 blocks, which figure can she build?
   a. 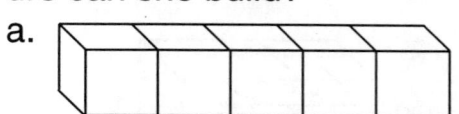
   b. 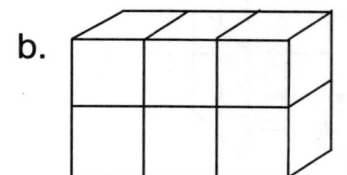
   c. 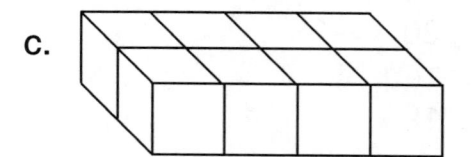
   d.

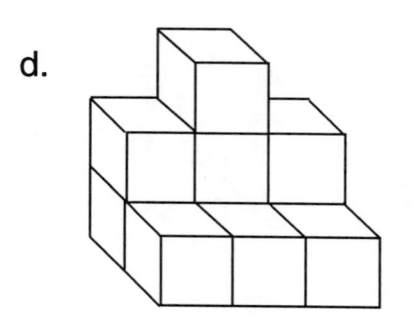

CHAPTER 11
COORDINATE PLANES, TRANSLATIONS, REFLECTIONS, AND ROTATIONS

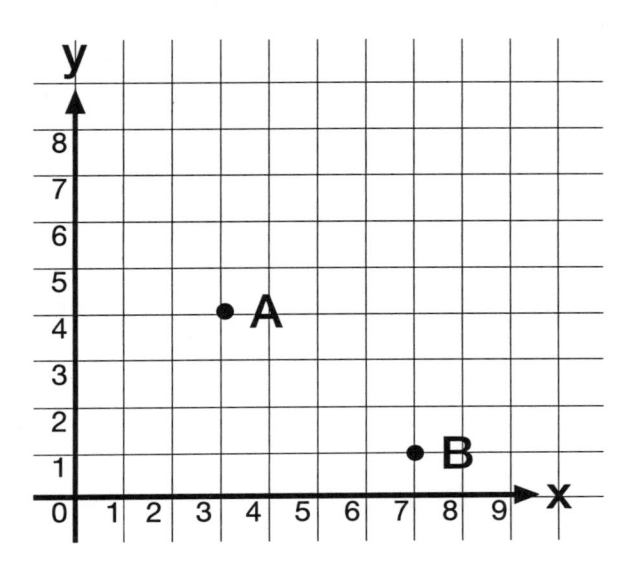

This is an example of a coordinate plane.

A coordinate plane contains:
1. a horizontal axis (left-right) called x-axis
2. a vertical axis (up-down) called y-axis
3. 0 (zero), where the x-axis and y-axis cross
4. x-axis and y-axis that are numbered
5. points that are named by letters (A, B)

ORDERED PAIRS IN COORDINATE PLANES

In the coordinate plane pictured above A = (3, 4) and B = (7, 1).

An ordered pair tells where a point is located on the coordinate plane. The first number is the x-axis, and the second number is the y-axis.

EXAMPLES

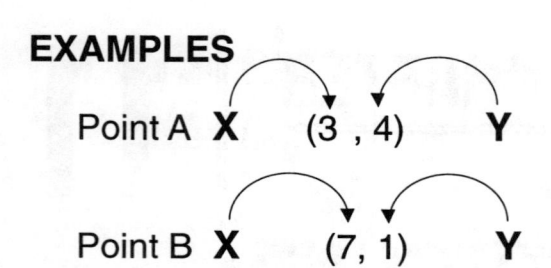

Point A X (3 , 4) Y   The 3 is 3 blocks to the right of 0 along
                            the x-axis, then 4 blocks up on the y-axis.

Point B X (7, 1) Y   The 7 is 7 blocks to the right of 0 along the
                            x-axis, then 1 block up on the y-axis.

PRACTICE

Write the ordered pair for each letter on the graph.

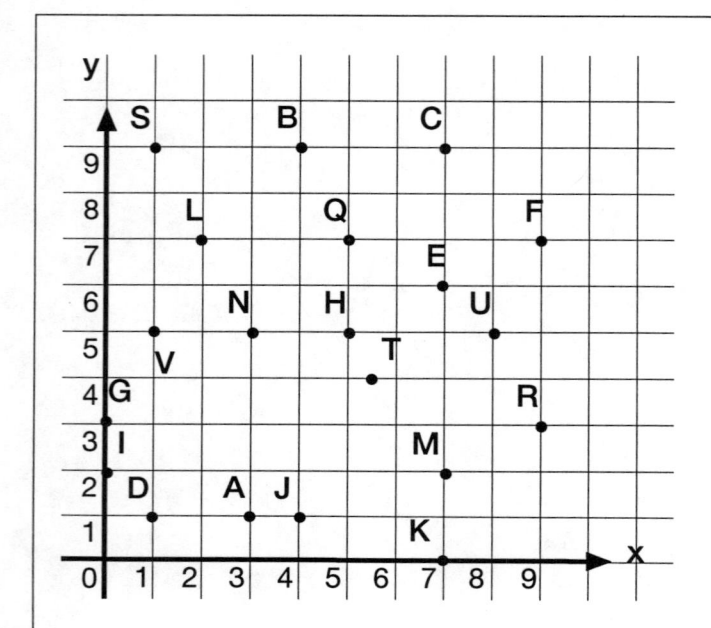

1. A _____
2. B _____
3. C _____
4. D _____
5. E _____

6. F _____
7. G _____
8. H _____
9. I _____
10. J _____

11. K _____
12. L _____
13. M _____
14. N _____
15. Q _____

16. R _____
17. S _____
18. T _____
19. U _____
20. V _____

TRANSLATING, REFLECTING, ROTATING, STRETCHING, AND SHRINKING FIGURES

To <u>translate</u> a figure, move it right, left, up, down, or a combination of these.

EXAMPLES:

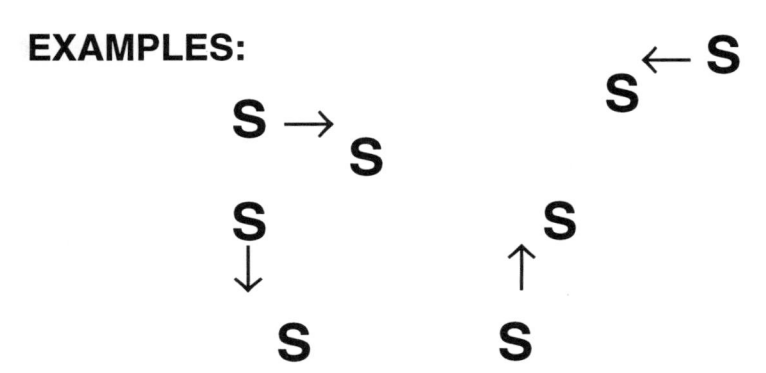

To <u>reflect</u> a figure about a line, the figure is drawn backwards (like a mirror image).

EXAMPLES:

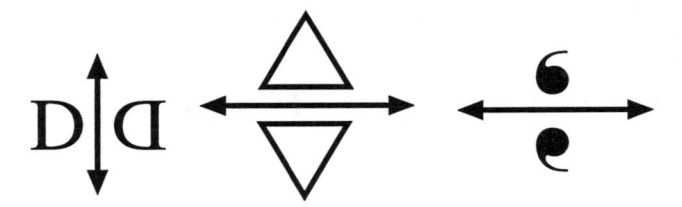

To <u>rotate</u> a figure, turn it in quarter turns like a clock.

EXAMPLES:

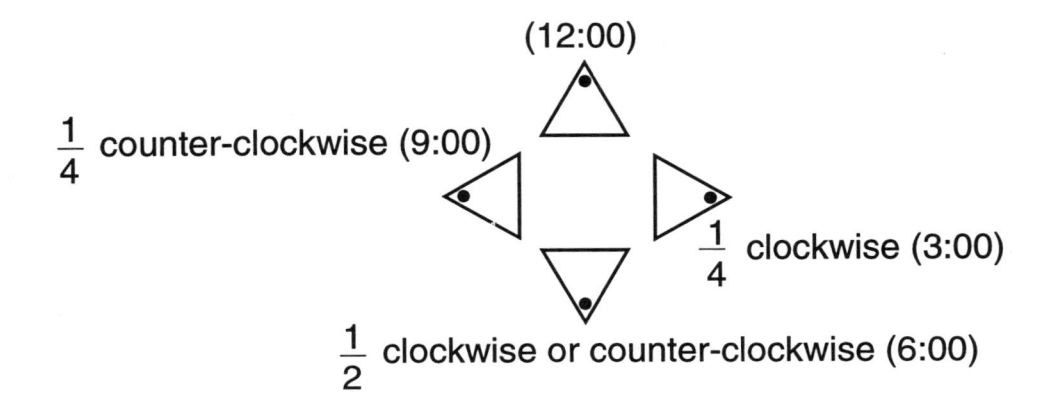

(12:00)

$\frac{1}{4}$ counter-clockwise (9:00)

$\frac{1}{4}$ clockwise (3:00)

$\frac{1}{2}$ clockwise or counter-clockwise (6:00)

Copyright © 1999 Contemporary Publishing Company of Raleigh, Inc.

To <u>stretch</u> a figure, pull certain sections or corners in a given direction.
EXAMPLE:

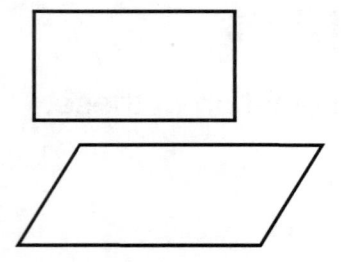

Stretch this figure by pulling two corners.

To <u>shrink</u> a figure, draw the same figure, just smaller.
EXAMPLE:

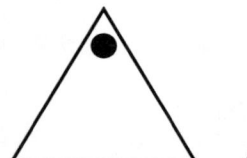

GRAPHING FIGURES

What shape is made when you graph (1, 1), (1, 4), (4, 4), (4, 1) in a coordinate plane? (Connect the points.)

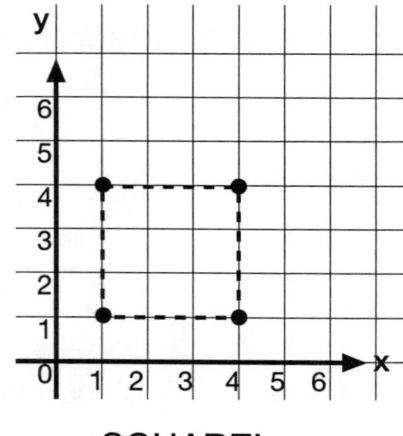

SQUARE!

PRACTICE

Draw a translation for each figure.

1. L (Translate to left.)

2. W (Translate down.)

3. O (Translate down and right.)

4. X (Translate left and up.)

5. V (Translate to right.)

Draw the reflection about the line.

6. S ←—→

7. W ←—→

8. X ←—→

9. △ ↕

10. ≳ ←—→

11. Oo ↕

12. L ↕

13. ▯ ↕

Rotate this figure.

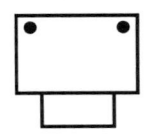

14. ¼ turn clockwise

15. ¼ turn counterclockwise

16. ½ turn clockwise

17. ½ turn counterclockwise

Copyright © 1999 Contemporary Publishing Company of Raleigh, Inc.

Stretch each figure by pulling 2 corners.

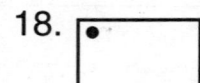

18.

19.

Shrink each figure.

20.

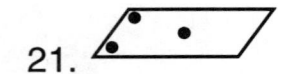

22.

21.

23.

Use this graph to answer questions 24-28.

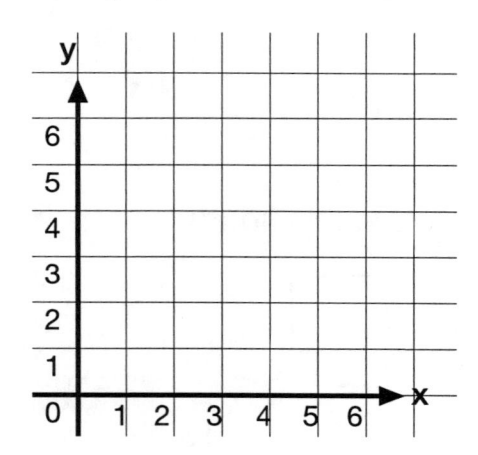

What shape is made when you graph these points on a coordinate plane and connect the points?

24. (1, 2), (3, 5), (5, 2) _____

25. (5, 4), (5, 2), (1, 2), (1, 4) _____

26. (2, 3), (5, 3), (5, 1) _____

27. (2, 2), (6, 2), (4, 4), (0, 4) _____

28. (5, 4), (5, 6), (3, 4), (3, 6) _____

REDUCING AND ENLARGING FIGURES

Remember that similar figures are figures that look the same, but are different sizes.

You can make a figure that is smaller than another by dividing its measurements.

EXAMPLE

Make a similar figure (smaller) by dividing all sides by 2.

$\dfrac{8 \text{ units}}{2} = 4 \text{ units}$ $\dfrac{10 \text{ units}}{2} = 5 \text{ units}$ $\dfrac{6 \text{ units}}{2} = 3 \text{ units}$

Now draw your new figure. (8 is now 4, 10 is now 5, and 6 is now 3.)

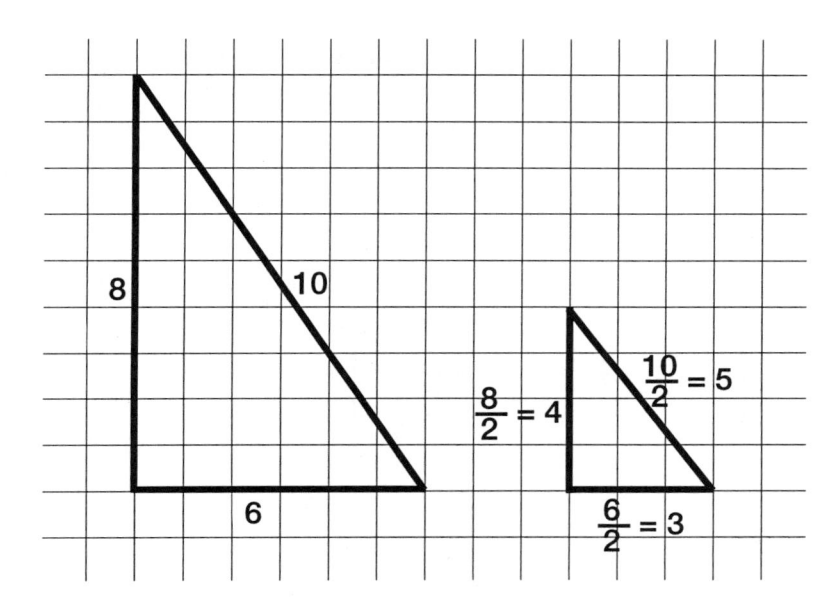

EXAMPLE

Make a similar figure (larger) by multiplying all sides by 2.

4 units × 2 = 8 units   6 units × 2 = 12 units

Now draw your new figure. (6 units is now 12, and 4 units is now 8.)

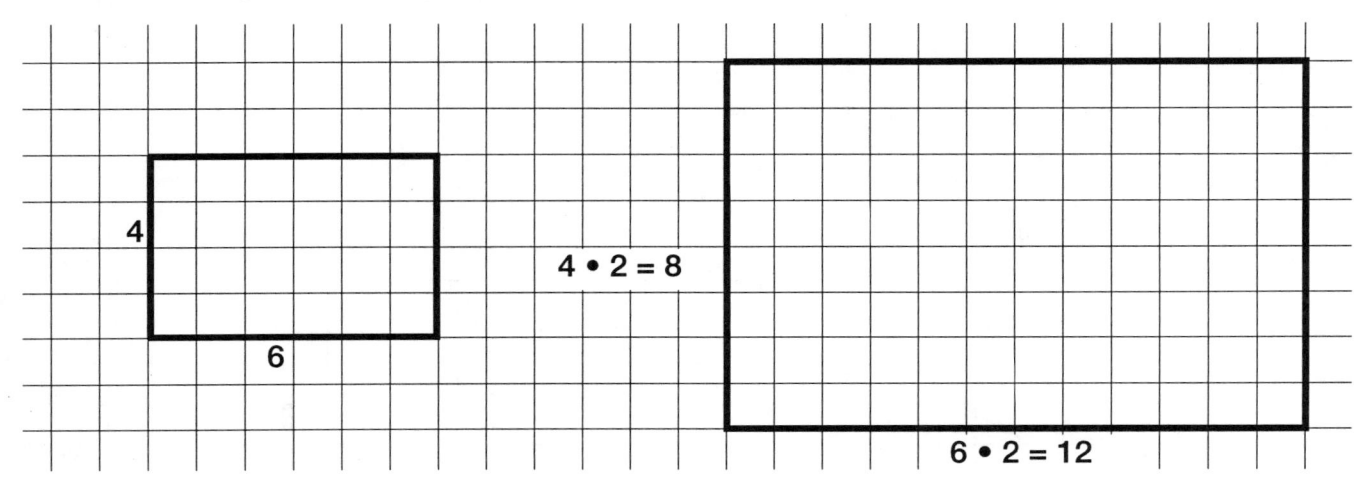

Copyright © 1999 Contemporary Publishing Company of Raleigh, Inc.

PRACTICE

On the graph paper, draw this figure smaller by dividing by:

1. 2

2. 4

On the graph paper, draw the same figure larger by multiplying by:

3. 2

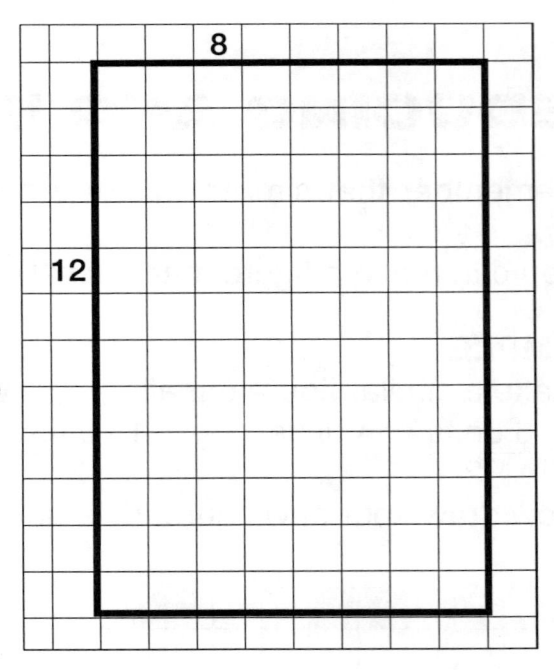

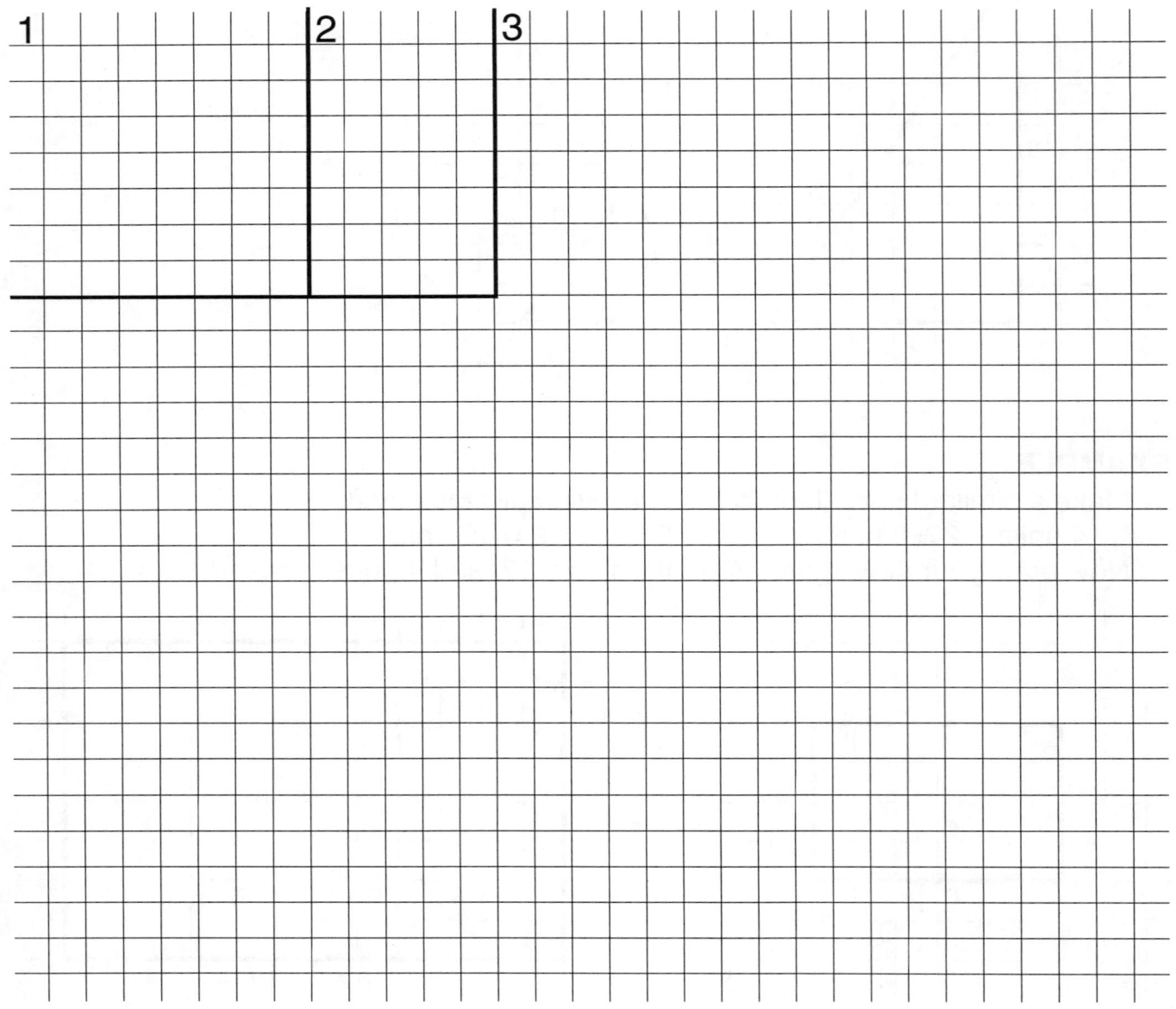

On the graph paper, draw this figure smaller by dividing by:

4. 2

5. 4

On the graph paper, draw the same figure larger by multiplying by:

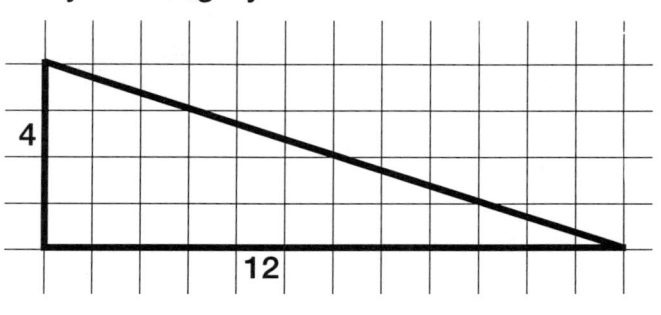

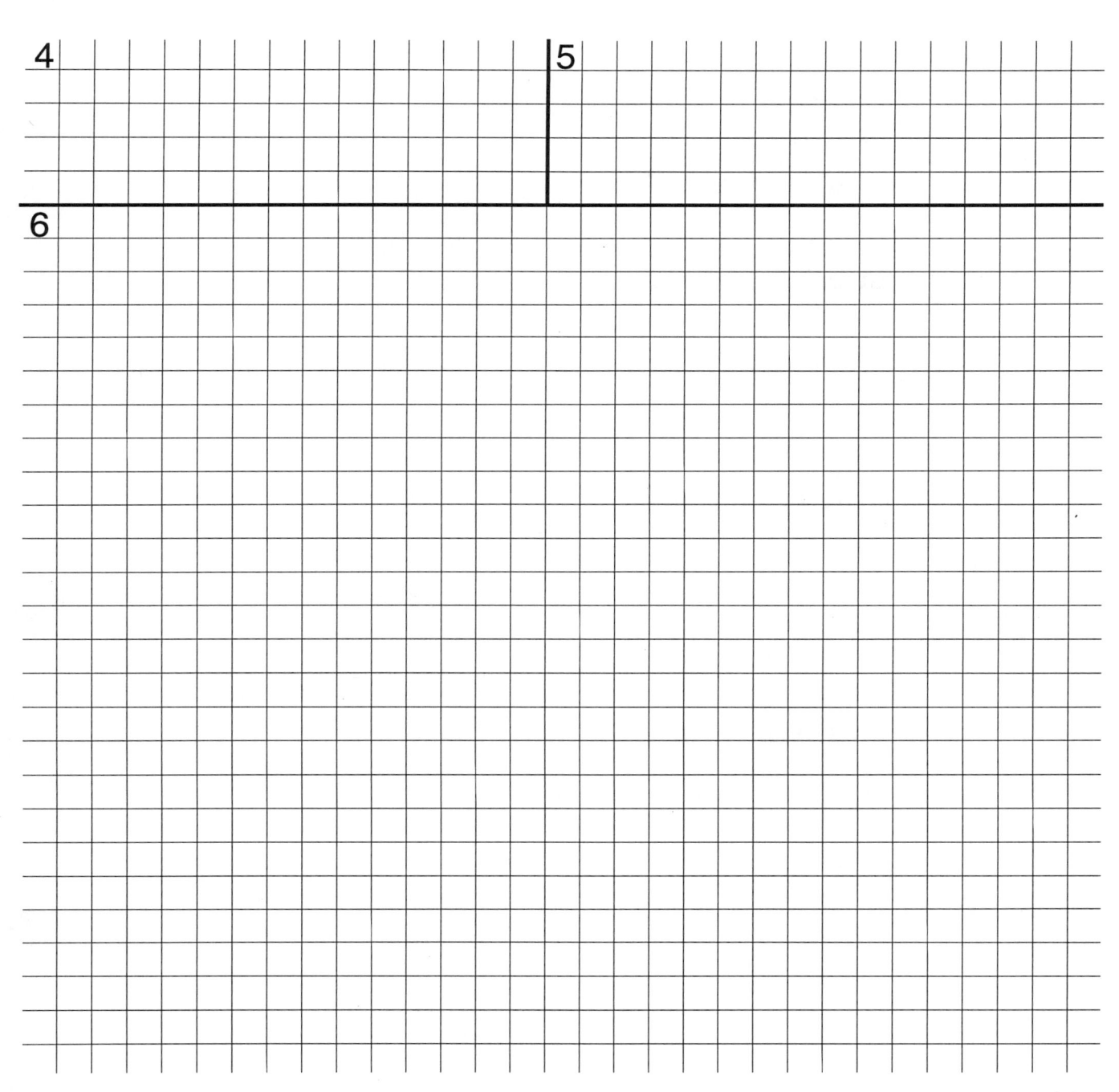

6. 2

147

REVIEW

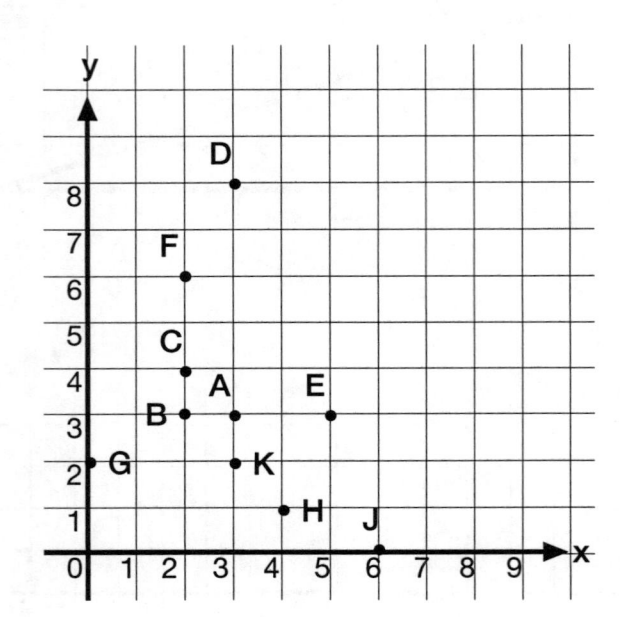

1. What ordered pair represents point J?
   a. (0, 6)
   b. (6, 0)
   c. (6, 6)
   d. (0, 0)

2. Which point has the ordered pair (2, 6)?
   a. J
   b. B
   c. E
   d. F

3. Point D is represented by what ordered pair?
   a. (3, 3)
   b. (3, 8)
   c. (8, 3)
   d. (3, –2)

4. (0, 2) is the ordered pair for point ___.
   a. B
   b. H
   c. J
   d. G

5. Which point has the ordered pair (5, 3)?
   a. B
   b. E
   c. F
   d. A

6. What is the ordered pair for point H?
   a. (4, 1)
   b. (1, 4)
   c. (6, 0)
   d. (0, 6)

7. (2, 4) is the ordered pair for point _____.
   a. J
   b. H
   c. K
   d. C

8. (3, 8) is the ordered pair for point ___.
   a. C
   b. D
   c. F
   d. B

9. Which of these is an example of translation?
   a. ≷→W
   b. ≷→≶
   c. W→
         W
   d. ≷→M

10. Which of the following shows a reflection about a line?
    a. B ↕ ᙠ
    b. B ↕ B
    c. B ↕
         B
    d. B ↕
         ᗺ

11. Which of the following is a reflection of this shape?
    a.
    b.
    c.
    d.

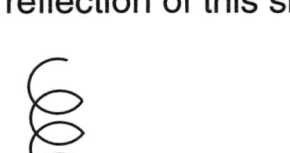

12. Which of these is an example of rotation?
    a.
    b.
    c.
    d.

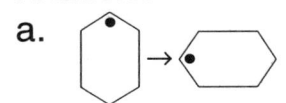

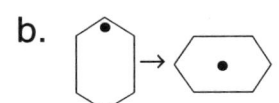

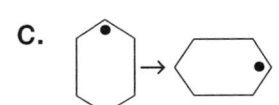

13. If the tree is E (east), what direction would the tree be if the picture was rotated ½ turn clockwise?

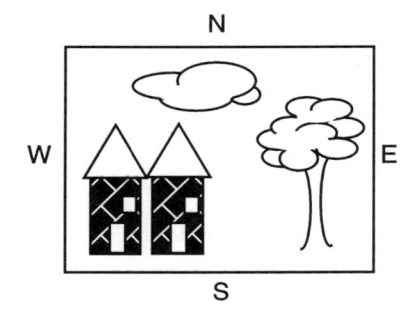

    a. north
    b. east
    c. west
    d. south

14. Which of the figures below shows this figure stretched at two corners?

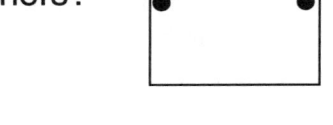

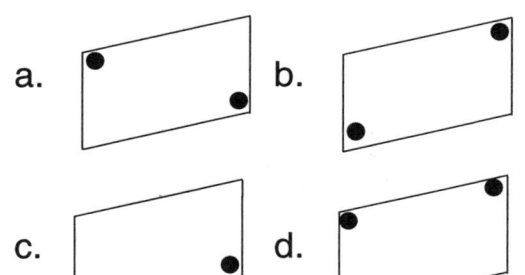

    a.
    b.
    c.
    d.

15. What would this line look like if it shrunk?

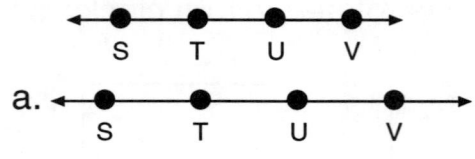

   S T U V

   a. S T U V
   b. S T U V
   c. T U V S
   d. S T U V

16. This ribbon is painted on one side.

   What would this piece of ribbon look like if it were twisted one time?

   a.
   b.
   c.
   d.

17. If you added a fourth point in the coordinate plane to form a rectangle, what would be its coordinates?

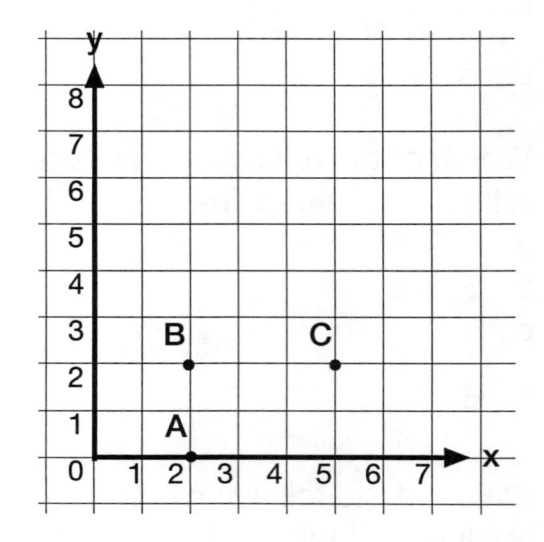

   a. (3, 3)
   b. (5, 0)
   c. (2, 2)
   d. (3, 2)

18. What shape is made if you graph these points on this coordinate plane?
   (1, 2), (5, 2), (3, 1)

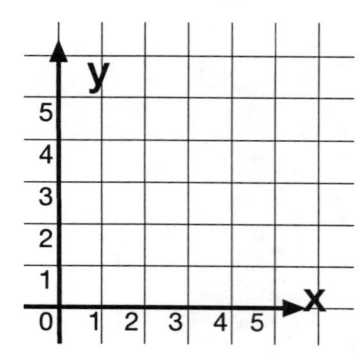

   a. triangle
   b. square
   c. rectangle
   d. prism

CHAPTER 12

TABLES, GRAPHS, MAPS, THERMOMETERS, AND CALENDARS

GRAPHS

There are 3 kinds of graphs that are used to compare data. They are line, bar, and circle.

EXAMPLES

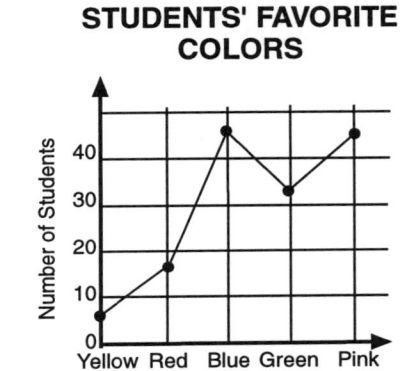

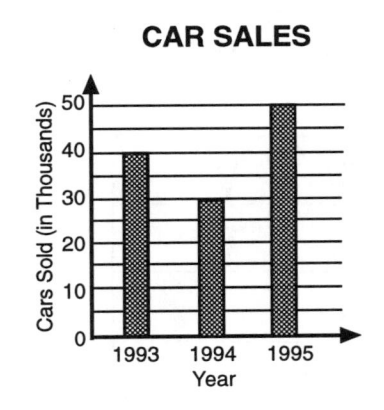

STUDENTS' FAVORITE COLORS

LINE GRAPH

CAR SALES

BAR GRAPH

MONTHLY BILLS

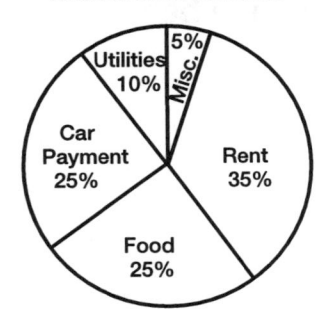

CIRCLE GRAPH

   Line and bar graphs have titles. They have labels on the horizontal (left-to-right) axis and the vertical (up-and-down) axis.
   Circle graphs have titles. They show information that equals to 100% when the parts of the circle are added together.

TABLES

Tables have titles, rows (Scout's name) and columns (weeks, total).

TICKET SALES

SCOUT'S NAME	WEEK 1	WEEK 2	WEEK 3	TOTAL
Mary	0	15	32	47
Sue	16	24	29	69
Janet	8	0	30	38

EXAMPLES

ICE CREAM	CHILDREN'S FAVORITE
Vanilla	🍦🍦
Chocolate	🍦🍦🍦
Strawberry	🍦🍦🍦
Lemon	🍦(half)
Cherry	🍦

🍦 = 10 children

How many children liked chocolate the best?

3 🍦 = 3 × 10 = 30

The answer is 30.

How many children liked lemon?

🍦 = 10 so (half) = 10 ÷ 2 = 5

The answer is 5.

152

TIMETABLES

Timetables are schedules for buses, trains, or planes that give you arrival and departure times.

EXAMPLES

BOSTON TO NEW YORK	
Boston	8:00 A.M.
Chestnut Hill	8:15 A.M.
Framingham	8:45 A.M.
Worchester	9:20 A.M.
Manchester	10:00 A.M.
Hartford	10:20 A.M.
New Haven	11:00 A.M.
Bridgeport	11:30 A.M.
New Rochelle	12:05 P.M.
New York	12:30 P.M.

What time does the bus leave Boston?

The answer is 8:00 A.M.

Where does the bus stop after it leaves Hartford?

The answer is New Haven.

PRACTICE

1. Draw a bar graph to show the number of sofas Don sold from January to December.

    January – 10   May – 31   September – 19
    February – 8   June – 20   October – 12
    March – 23   July – 17   November – 7
    April – 16   August – 21   December – 29

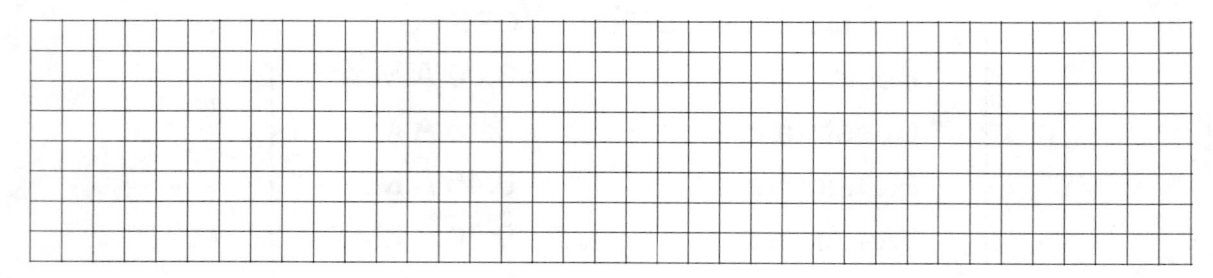

2. Draw a line graph to show the number of people surveyed who like a specific kind of ice cream.

    Chocolate – 55   Pineapple – 10
    Vanilla – 60   Walnut – 2
    Strawberry – 30   Lemon – 21
    Raspberry – 15
    Mint – 5

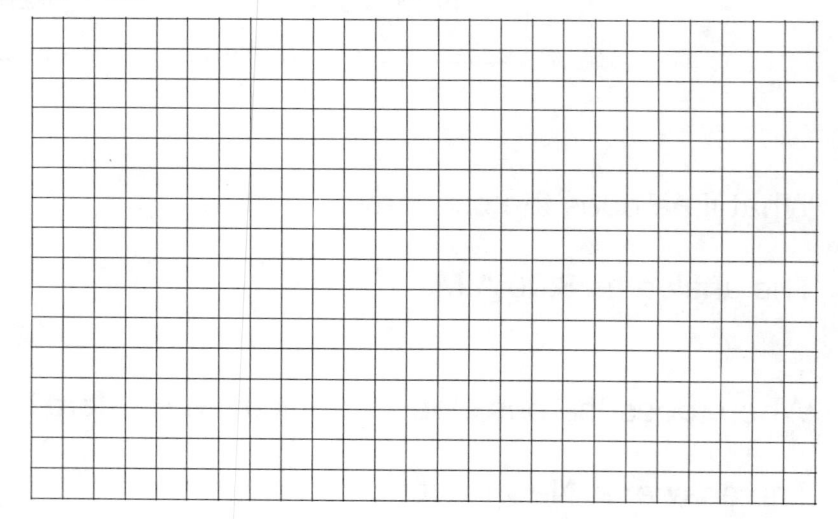

3. Draw a table to show how many magazines were sold each day by a group of boys. (Make a total column.)

	Monday	Tuesday	Wednesday
John	30	16	18
Roy	80	34	25
Chester	21	92	38

MILEAGE MAPS

A mileage map gives the distance between certain cities, towns, places, etc.

EXAMPLE

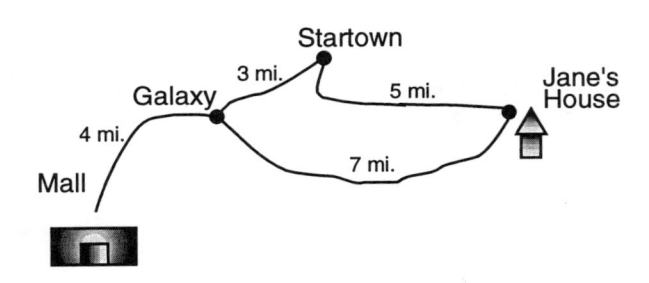

What is the distance from Jane's house to the mall using the shortest route?

Route A	Route B
7 mi.	5 mi.
+ 4 mi.	3 mi.
11 mi.	+ 4 mi.
	12 mi.

The shortest route is 11 miles.

THERMOMETERS

Thermometers measure the degrees of hotness or coldness.

EXAMPLES

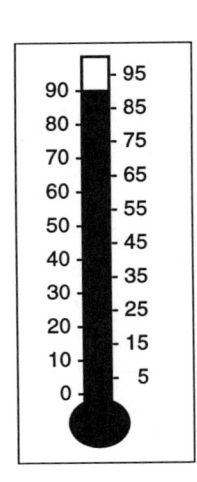

1. What is the temperature?_____
The answer is 90°.

2. What type of clothes would you wear on a day with this temperature?_____
Since the temperature is 90°, you should wear some type of summer clothing.

155

CALENDARS

A calendar shows the months of the year and days of the month.

EXAMPLES

\	\	\	MARCH	\	\	\
S	M	T	W	T	F	S
	1	2	3	4	5	6
7	8	9	10	11	12	13
14	15	16	17	18	19	20
21	22	23	24	25	26	27
28	29	30	31			

1. What day is March 18? _____

The answer is Thursday.

2. How many Tuesdays are in March? _____

The answer is 5.

PRACTICE

Use the map below to answer each question.

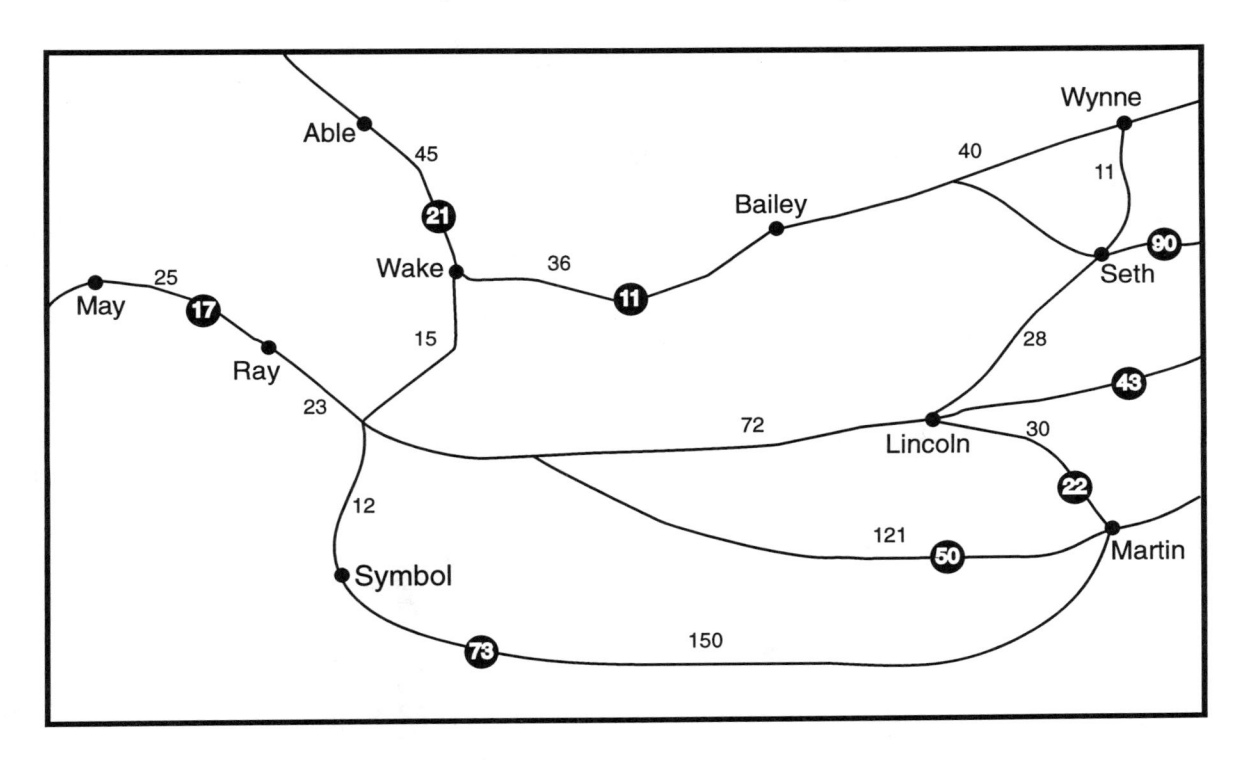

1. What is the distance from May to Ray? _____

2. What is the distance from May to Symbol? _____

3. What is the shortest distance from May to Lincoln? _____

4. What is the shortest distance from May to Martin? _____

5. What is the shortest distance from Lincoln to Ray? _____

6. What is the distance from Ray to Wake? _____

7. What is the distance from Symbol to Lincoln on ⑦③ and ㉒? _____

8. What is the distance from Wake to Bailey? _____

9. What is the distance from Wake to Wynne? _____

10. What is the distance from Wake to Able? _____

(continued on next page)

11. What is the distance from Wake to Seth on ⑪ and ⑨⓪? _____

12. What is the distance from Able to Wynne? _____

13. What is the shortest route from Ray to Martin on ⑰ and ⑦③? _____

14. What is the longest route from Wake to Seth? _____

15. What is the shortest route from Able to Lincoln? _____

Use these thermometers to answer #16–20.

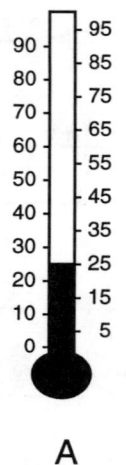

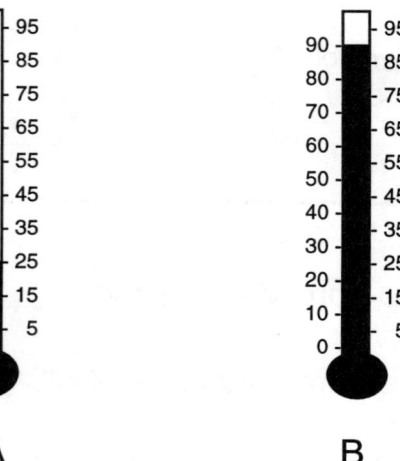

A   B

16. What is the temperature on thermometer A? _____

17. What is the temperature on thermometer B? _____

18. What type of clothing would you choose to wear if you lived where thermometer A was located? _____

19. What type of clothing would you choose to wear if you lived where thermometer B was located? _____

20. What is the season for thermometer B? _____

Use this calendar to answer questions 21–25.

			JULY			
S	M	T	W	T	F	S
				1	2	3
4	5	6	7	8	9	10
11	12	13	14	15	16	17
18	19	20	21	22	23	24
25	26	27	28	29	30	31

21. How many full weeks are in July? _____

22. What day of the week is July 4? _____

23. How many Saturdays are in July? _____

24. What date is the last day of the month? _____

25. What day is the first day of the month? _____

Copyright © 1999 Contemporary Publishing Company of Raleigh, Inc.

REVIEW

Use the bar graph to answer 1–6.

TIRE SALES

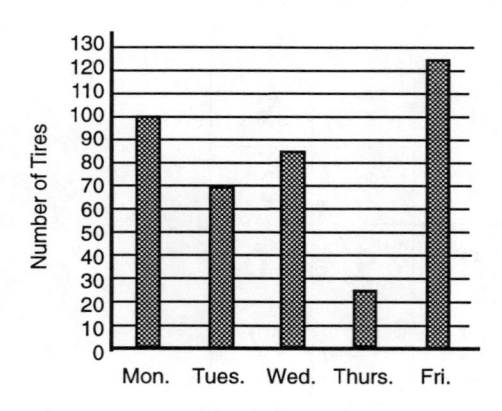

1. How many tires were sold on Friday?
   a. 130
   b. 125
   c. 120
   d. 85

2. 85 tires were sold on what day?
   a. Monday
   b. Tuesday
   c. Wednesday
   d. Thursday

3. How many more tires were sold on Friday than on Tuesday?
   a. 195
   b. 70
   c. 125
   d. 55

4. Based on the graph, which statement is true?
   a. More tires were sold on Friday than any other day.
   b. The amount of tires sold on Tuesday was the greatest.
   c. Less tires were sold on Monday than on any other day.
   d. Thursday was the best day to sell tires.

5. Which statement about Thursday is not true?
   a. Thursday was the poorest sales day.
   b. Thursday's sales were 1/4 of Wednesday's sales.
   c. Thursday's sales were 1/6 of Friday's sales.
   d. Thursday had the greatest amount of tires sold.

6. To the nearest hundred, what is the best estimate of the number of tires sold in the 5 day period?
   a. 305
   b. 300
   c. 504
   d. 400

Use the line graph to answer 7–12.

LONG DISTANCE PHONE CALLS

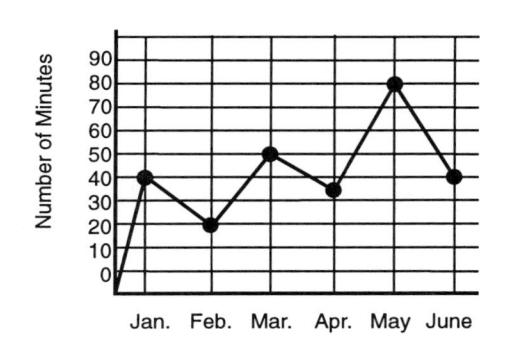

7. What information is given on the horizontal (left to right) axis?
   a. Long Distance Phone Calls
   b. Number of Minutes
   c. Months
   d. 0–90

8. What statement is true about this graph?
   a. The number of minutes used for long distance increased each month.
   b. Every other month there was a decrease in minutes from the previous month.
   c. Long distance minutes decreased each month.
   d. June had more long distance minutes than May.

9. Which month has the greatest number of minutes?
   a. January
   b. May
   c. February
   d. June

10. Which month has the smallest number of minutes?
    a. January
    b. February
    c. March
    d. April

11. To the nearest hundred, what is the best estimate of the number of minutes used from January to June?
    a. 200
    b. 300
    c. 260
    d. 100

12. How many minutes were used in March and April?
    a. 260
    b. 60
    c. 85
    d. 115

Use this chart to answer 13–16.

MAGAZINE SALES

DAY	CHARLES	JOHN
Monday	16	14
Tuesday	7	11
Wednesday	9	22
Thursday	11	14
Friday	8	9

13. Find the total number of magazines Charles sold.
    a. 47
    b. 50
    c. 51
    d. 48

14. How many more magazines were sold on Monday than on Thursday?
    a. 5
    b. 55
    c. 2
    d. 10

15. How many more magazines did John sell than Charles?
    a. 121
    b. 70
    c. 51
    d. 19

16. What is the total number of magazines sold by John and Charles?
    a. 121
    b. 70
    c. 51
    d. 19

Use the circle graph to answer 17–21.

COLLEGE EXPENSES

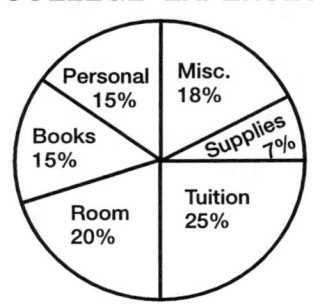

- Personal 15%
- Misc. 18%
- Books 15%
- Supplies 7%
- Room 20%
- Tuition 25%

17. What part of college expense is tuition?
    a. 15
    b. 18
    c. 20
    d. 25

18. Books are __% of college expenses.
    a. 20%
    b. 15%
    c. 7%
    d. 25%

19. What 2 expenses are the same?
    a. room and tuition
    b. miscellaneous and supplies
    c. room and miscellaneous
    d. books and personal

20. Which expense is less than books?
    a. tuition
    b. supplies
    c. personal
    d. room

21. What is true about college expenses?
    a. Tuition is the most expensive part of college expenses.
    b. Rooms are the cheapest part of college expenses.
    c. Supplies and miscellaneous make up 50% of college expenses.
    d. All college expenses are equal.

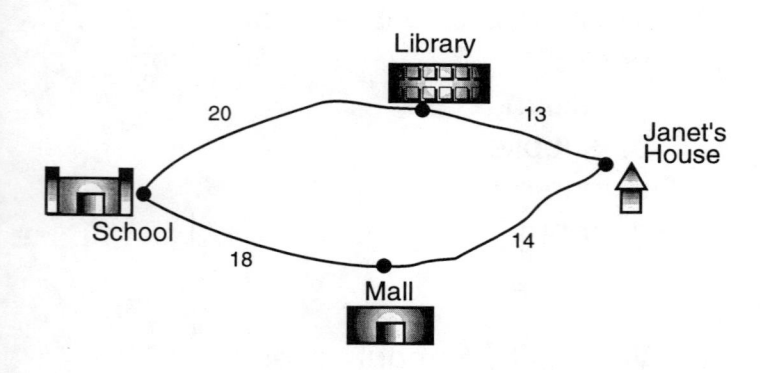

22. How far is the shortest route from Janet's house to school?
    a. 32
    b. 18
    c. 27
    d. 33

23. What clothes would Guy choose to wear if the daytime temperature is registered on this thermometer?

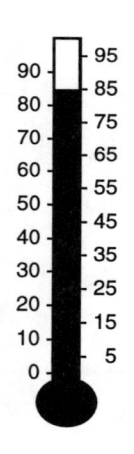

    a. wool coat
    b. sweatshirt and long pants
    c. sweater and jeans
    d. shirt and shorts

Route 15

Monday through Friday

Downtown	7:20 A.M.
Taylor Ave	7:26 A.M.
Mann Road	7:31 A.M.
Blue Street	7:33 A.M.
Jay Ave	7:36 A.M.
Parkway	7:40 A.M.

24. What time does the bus leave downtown?
    a. Route 15
    b. Monday through Friday
    c. 7:20 A.M.
    d. 7:40 A.M.

25. What stop is after Blue Street?
    a. Mann Road
    b. Downtown
    c. Parkway
    d. Jay Avenue

			AUGUST			
S	M	T	W	T	F	S
1	2	3	4	5	6	7
8	9	10	11	12	13	14
15	16	17	18	19	20	21
22	23	24	25	26	27	28
29	30	31				

26. How many days are in August?
    a. 4
    b. 31
    c. 12
    d. 15

27. What day of the week is August 23?
    a. Monday
    b. Friday
    c. Sunday
    d. Saturday

28. How many Sundays are in August?
    a. 4
    b. 6
    c. 5
    d. 3

Copyright © 1999 Contemporary Publishing Company of Raleigh, Inc.

CHAPTER 13

NUMBER PATTERNS

A pattern is something that is repeated. There are number patterns and geometric patterns.

EXAMPLES

NUMBER PATTERNS

2, 4, 6, 8, 10
$2 \xrightarrow{+2} 4 \xrightarrow{+2} 6 \xrightarrow{+2} 8 \xrightarrow{+2} 10$

Do you see a pattern? Starting with 2, add 2. Then add 2 to each number after that.

10, 20, 30, 40, 50
$10 \xrightarrow{+10} 20 \xrightarrow{+10} 30 \xrightarrow{+10} 40 \xrightarrow{+10} 50$

Do you see a pattern? Starting with 10, add 10. Then add 10 to each number after that.

ORDERED PAIRS

(10, 8), (9, 7), (8, 6)
$(10^{-1}, 8^{-1}), (9^{-1}, 7^{-1}), (8, 6)$

Do you see a pattern? Each coordinate (x and y) decreases by 1.

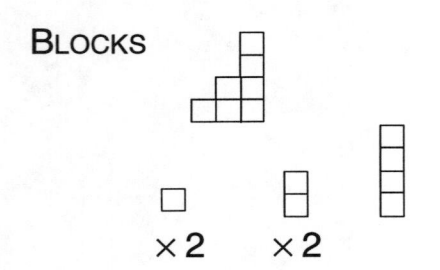

BLOCKS

Do you see a pattern? Each block is multiplied by 2.

×2   ×2

GEOMETRIC PATTERNS

△ □ ○ △ □ ○ △ □ ○
1 2 3 4 5 6 7 8 9

What is the correct shape for the 10th position? △ since △ follows ○.

☆ △ ☆ △ ☆ △ ☆ △
1 2 3 4 5 6 7 8

What is the correct shape for the 40th position? (Notice that ☆'s are odd and △'s are even.) 40 is even, so it will be a △.

EXAMPLE

Input	Output
0	2
1	3
2	4
3	5

If the output is 7, what is the input?

Pattern: Output − Input = 2
7 − 2 = 5

166 Copyright © 1999 Contemporary Publishing Company of Raleigh, Inc.

PRACTICE

Continue the pattern.

1. 1, 5, 9, 13, 17, _____, _____, _____

2. 2, 4, 6, 8, _____, _____, _____

3. △ △ ▢▢ △ △ _____, _____, _____

4. ☺ ☺ ☹ ☺ ☺ ☹ ☺ _____, _____, _____

5. 6, 7, 8, 9, _____, _____, _____

6. 12, 10, 8, 6, _____, _____, _____

7. ⊙ O ⊙ O ⊙ _____, _____, _____

8. 20, 30, 40, 50, _____, _____, _____

9. 100, 97, 94, 91, _____, _____, _____

10. 0, 1, 2, 3, _____, _____, _____

11. ● ◆ ● ◆ ● _____, _____, _____

12. (1, 1), (2, 2), (3, 3) _____, _____, _____

13. ▫, ▫▫, ▫▫▫, ▫▫▫▫ , _____, _____, _____

14. 10, 15, 20, 25, _____, _____, _____

15. 40, 39, 38, 37, _____, _____, _____

16. ▫ , ⌸, ⌻ _____, _____, _____

17. 1, 2, 4, 7, 11, _____, _____, _____

18. (2, 4), (3, 5), (4, 6) _____, _____, _____

19. ▭, ▯, ▭, ▯, ▭, _____, _____, _____

20. 103, 106, 109, 112, _____, _____, _____

SORTING BY PATTERNS

EXAMPLE

How would you sort this group of figures?

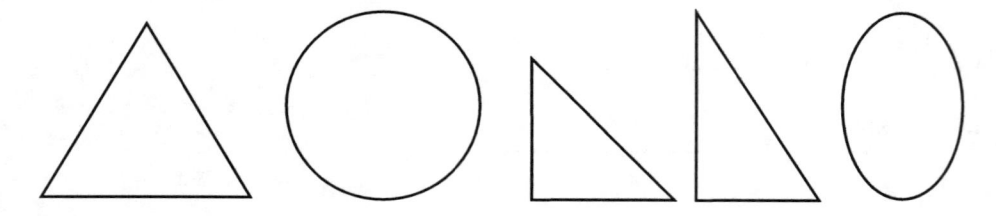

Put figures with angles together.

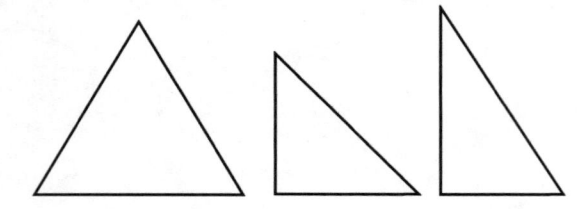

Put figures with no angles together.

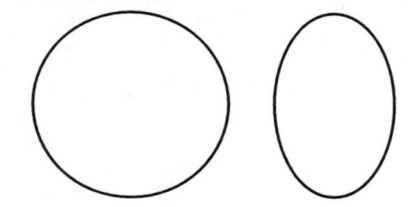

PRACTICE

Sort each group of figures.

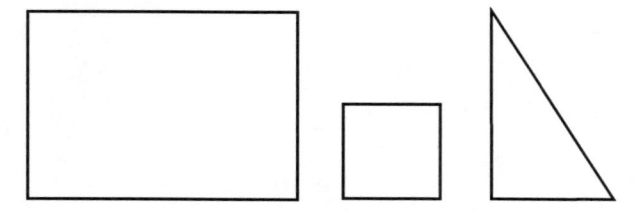

1.

2.

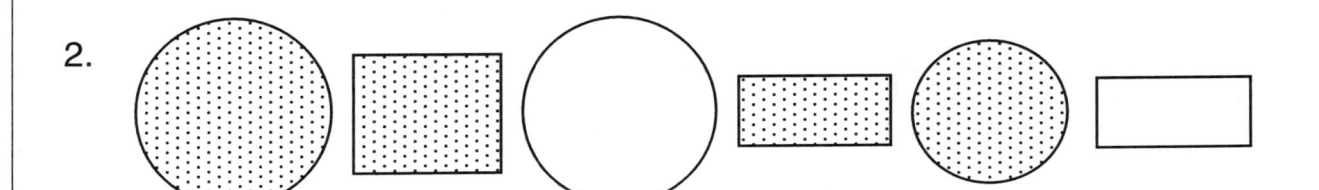

3.

4.

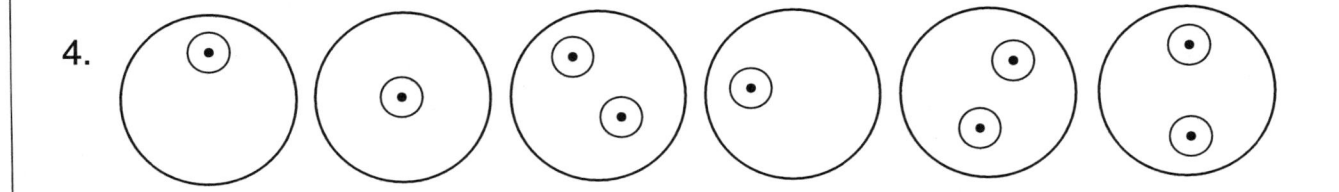

(continued on next page)

5.

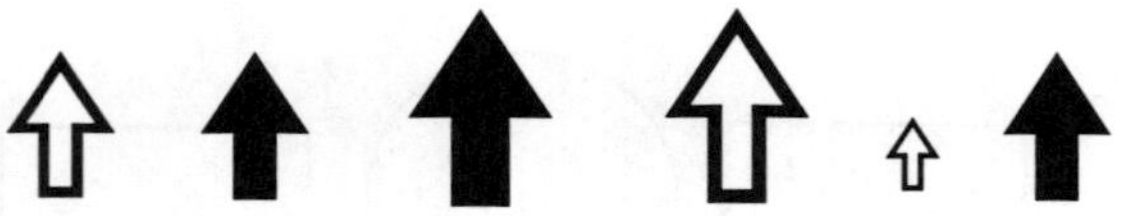

6.

7.

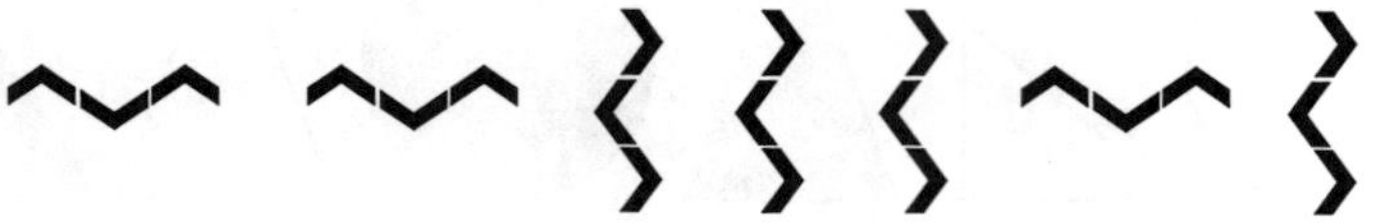

Give the reason why these figures were grouped together.

8.

9.

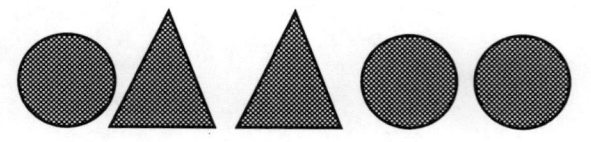

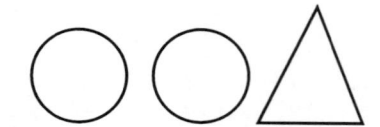

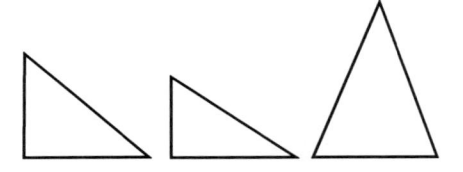

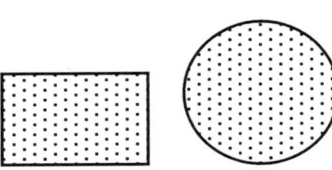

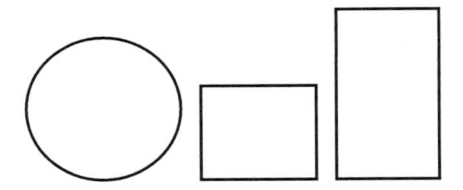

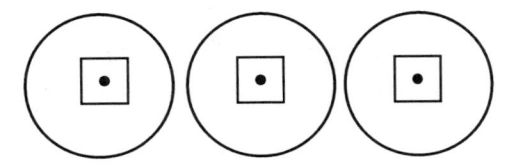

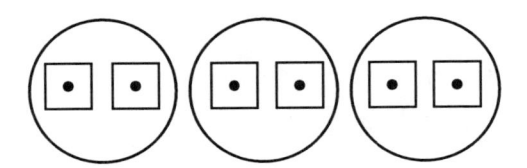

10.

11.

12.

REVIEW

1. What are the next 3 terms in this sequence? 109, 104, 99, 94
   a. 93, 92, 91
   b. 89, 84, 79
   c. 95, 91, 90
   d. 92, 90, 88

2. What is the next ordered pair in this sequence?
   (10, 7), (8, 5), (6, 3)
   a. (5, 2)
   b. (4, 1)
   c. (5, 4)
   d. (4, 0)

3. In the sequence 15, ___, 45, 60, what is the missing number?
   a. 25
   b. 20
   c. 30
   d. 35

4. What are the next 3 terms in this sequence? 20, 19, 18, 17
   a. 16, 15, 14
   b. 15, 14, 13
   c. 15, 13, 11
   d. 15, 10, 9

5. Is this an arithmetic sequence? Do you find a pattern? 1, 3, 5, 7
   a. yes
   b. no

6. What is the next fraction in this sequence? $\frac{1}{3}$, $\frac{1}{4}$, $\frac{1}{5}$
   a. $\frac{1}{2}$
   b. $\frac{1}{7}$
   c. $\frac{1}{6}$
   d. $\frac{1}{1}$

7. What is the twelfth number in this sequence? 11, 18, 25, 32
   a. 60
   b. 88
   c. 81
   d. 95

8. What is the next shape in this sequence? ■●●■●●■●
   a. ■
   b. ●
   c. ●●
   d. ■●

9. What is the 10th shape in this sequence? ✳✪✳✪✳✪
   a. ✪✪
   b. ✳
   c. ✪
   d. ✳✳

10. If the input is 6, what is the output?

Input	1	2	3	4
Output	3	6	9	12

   a. 3
   b. 2
   c. 18
   d. 20

11. If the output is 13, what is the input?

Input	Output
0	1
1	4
2	7

   a. 5
   b. 6
   c. 7
   d. 4

12. Angelo has 7 yellow bottle caps, 8 orange bottle caps, and 9 silver bottle caps. He wants to make a pattern on a circular board with the three colors in this order—yellow, orange, silver. What is the greatest number of bottle caps that he can use and continue this pattern?
   a. 24
   b. 15
   c. 21
   d. 17

13. Study the chart. What is the value of b when a = 2?
   a. 1
   b. 0
   c. 3
   d. 10

a	b
9	7
8	6
7	5
6	4

14. What are the next 3 terms in this sequence?
      10, 20, 30, __, __, __
   a. 31, 32, 33
   b. 35, 40, 45
   c. 35, 45, 55
   d. 40, 50, 60

15. What is the pattern?

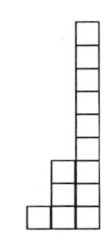

   a. + 3
   b. × 3
   c. × 2
   d. − 3

16. How do you find the next term in this sequence? 5, 15, 25, 35, ___
   a. Add 15.
   b. Multiply by 5.
   c. Multiply by 3.
   d. Add 10.

17. What is the next term in this sequence?

    ❖ ❖ ❖ ◆ ◆ ❖ ❖ ❖ ◆

    a. ❖
    b. ◆
    c. ◆◆
    d. ❖❖

18. What is the missing term?
    1, 3, 5, 7, 9, ___, 13
    a. 10
    b. 2
    c. 11
    d. 12

19. What are the next 3 terms? 47, 40, 33, 26, ___, ___, ___
    a. 20, 14, 8
    b. 33, 40, 47
    c. 25, 24, 23
    d. 19, 12, 5

20. H, T, H, T, HH, H, T, H, T, HH
    What is the next term?
    a. H
    b. T
    c. HH
    d. TT

21. Which of the following shapes would not be grouped together?
    a. 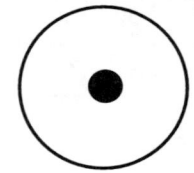
    b. 
    c. 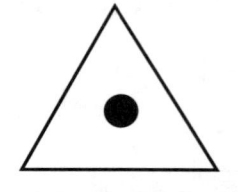
    d.

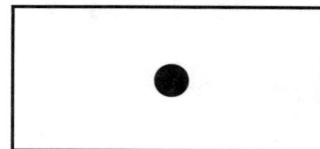

22. What would be a good rule for sorting these objects into two groups?

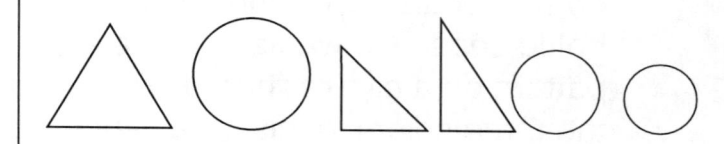

    a. large circles in one group, large triangles in the other
    b. white circles in one group, striped triangles in the other
    c. triangles in one group, circles in the other
    d. 2 circles in one group, one circle and three triangles in the other

174

23. What would most likely come next?

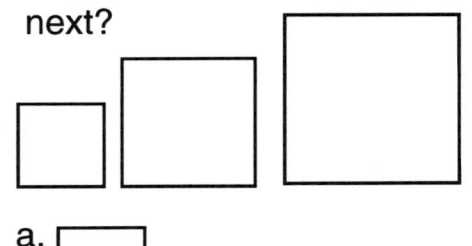

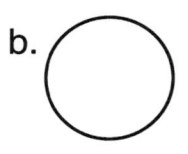

a.

b.

c.

d.

24. What number belongs in the empty box?

| 6 | 12 | ? | 24 | 30 |

   a. 20
   b. 13
   c. 18
   d. 15

25 What is the pattern?

   a. subtract 1
   b. add 2
   c. multiply by 2
   d. add 5

Practice Test 1
Use answer sheet provided in the back of this book.

1. Nasir had 30 inches of tape that will be divided into 5 pieces. What is the length of each piece?
   a. 15
   b. 6
   c. 35
   d. 25

2. How many blocks are shaded?

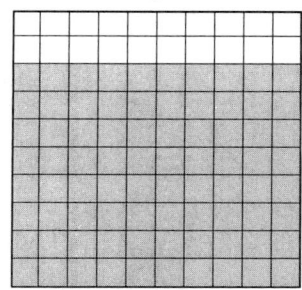

   a. 4
   b. 75
   c. 80
   d. 90

3. What is the time on this clock?

   a. 12:25
   b. 5:00
   c. 4:00
   d. 6:00

4. What fraction of the figures are stars?

   a. $\frac{3}{13}$
   b. $\frac{4}{13}$
   c. $\frac{6}{13}$
   d. $\frac{3}{3}$

5. Which angle is closest to 60°?
   a.
   b.
   c.
   d.

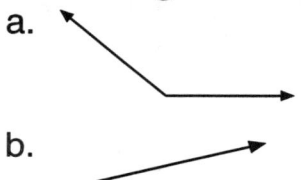

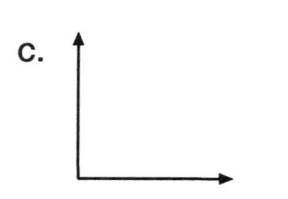

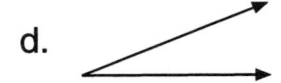

6. Which fraction is the smallest?
   a. $\frac{1}{2}$
   b. $\frac{1}{3}$
   c. $\frac{1}{5}$
   d. $\frac{1}{4}$

7.

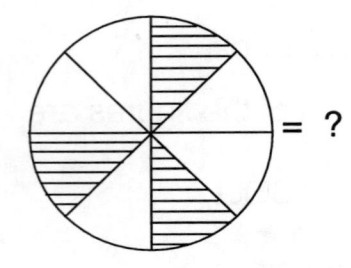

a. $\frac{5}{8}$
b. $\frac{8}{8}$
c. $\frac{2}{8}$
d. $\frac{3}{8}$

8. What would be the top view of this juice container?

a. (rectangle)
b. (square)
c. (ellipse)
d. (circle)

9. Scott bought a coat for $40.00. If he gave the cashier $100.00, how much change does he receive?
a. $140
b. $60
c. $50
d. $20

10. $7 \times 6 =$ __?
a. 49
b. 13
c. 42
d. 56

11. Charlotte saw a sign in the store window that advertised birthday cards $1.00 off regular price. How much would you pay for a card that regularly costs $2.00?
a. $1.50
b. $12.50
c. $1.00
d. $.50

12. Which of the following is an example of an obtuse angle?

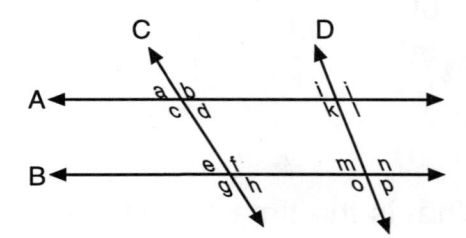

a. ∠a
b. ∠e
c. ∠i
d. ∠b

Copyright © 1999 Contemporary Publishing Company of Raleigh, Inc.

13. The perimeter of a rectangular bank is 30 ft. The length of one side of the bank is 10 ft. What is the width of the building?

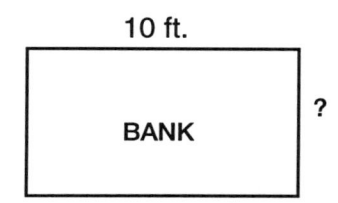

10 ft.

BANK ?

   a. 20 ft.
   b. 25 ft.
   c. 10 ft.
   d. 5 ft.

14. A large blue blanket measures 9 ft. by 8 ft. A small blue blanket measures 5 ft. by 3 ft. What is the difference in the areas of the two blankets?
   a. 57 ft.²
   b. 87 ft.²
   c. 114 ft.²
   d. 15 ft.²

15. If this pattern continues (10, 7, 4, . . .), what would be the next number?
   a. 0
   b. 7
   c. 1
   d. 10

16. Write ten thousand dollars in standard form.
   a. $1,000.00
   b. $10.00
   c. $100.00
   d. $10,000.00

17. What is the amount shown by these circles?

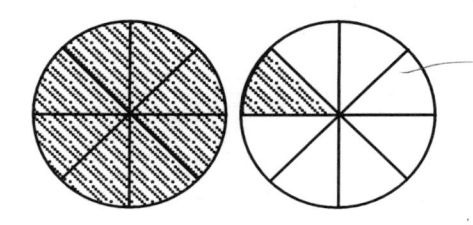

   a. $\dfrac{10}{8}$
   b. $\dfrac{1}{8}$
   c. $1\dfrac{7}{8}$
   d. $1\dfrac{1}{8}$

18. Which student had the largest piece of candy bar?
   a. $\dfrac{1}{2}$ (Janet)
   b. $\dfrac{7}{8}$ (Kaye)
   c. $\dfrac{3}{4}$ (Marsha)
   d. $\dfrac{5}{12}$ (Wally)

Copyright © 1999 Contemporary Publishing Company of Raleigh, Inc.

19. Which number is odd?
    a. 2
    b. 3
    c. 10
    d. 18

20. Which of the following is a set of equivalent fractions?
    a. ($1/2$, $1/3$, $1/7$)
    b. ($6/8$, $12/16$, $1/4$)
    c. ($1/2$, $6/12$, $12/24$)
    d. ($3/4$, $4/5$, $8/11$)

21. Who had the largest quantity?
    a. Bud   556 g
    b. Abby   550 g
    c. Jane   593 g
    d. Marlowe 450 g

22. What is the length of a rectangle with an area of 20 square yards and a width of 5 yds.? (A = lw)
    a. 100 yds.
    b. 55 yds.
    c. $\frac{1}{4}$ yd.
    d. 4 yds.

23. Which of the following is a sphere?
    a. a baseball
    b. a football
    c. a catcher's mitt
    d. a hotdog

24. Which one of these fractions is less than $1/4$?
    a. $\frac{1}{3}$
    b. $\frac{1}{2}$
    c. $\frac{1}{8}$
    d. $\frac{3}{8}$

25. Round $27.86 to the nearest dollar.
    a. $27.86
    b. $28.00
    c. $27.90
    d. $27.00

26. ☐ ÷ 4 = 9
    a. 28
    b. 13
    c. 5
    d. 36

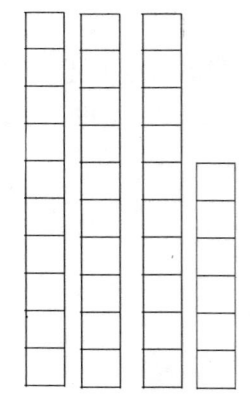

27. = _____.
    a. 20
    b. 36
    c. 306
    d. 204

Copyright © 1999 Contemporary Publishing Company of Raleigh, Inc.

		OCTOBER				
S	M	T	W	T	F	S
	1	2	3	4	5	6
7	8	9	10	11	12	13
14	15	16	17	18	19	20
21	22	23	24	25	26	27
28	29	30	31			

28. What day is October 10?
    a. Saturday
    b. Tuesday
    c. Wednesday
    d. Thursday

29. What could be the measurement for the width of this ring?

    a. 1 ½ meters
    b. 1 ½ centimeters
    c. 1 ½ grams
    d. 1 ½ milliliters

30. Which figure has right angles?
    a. 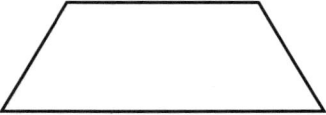
    b. 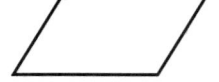
    c. 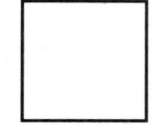
    d.

31. Study the patterns.

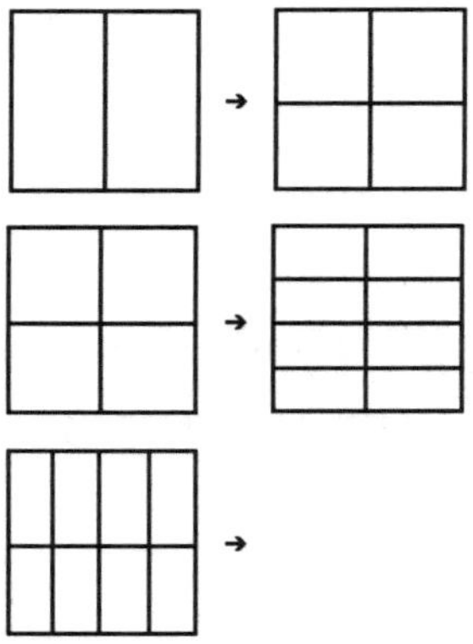

    Which figure completes the pattern?
    a. 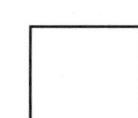
    b. 
    c. 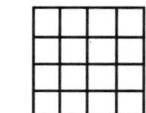
    d.

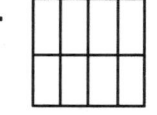

32. The points (1, 1), (1, 3), (6, 1), and (6, 3) are plotted on graph paper. What is the shape of the object when the points are connected?
   a. circle
   b. square
   c. triangle
   d. rectangle

33. Carolyn can read 15 words in 3 minutes. How many words can she read in 9 minutes?
   a. 135
   b. 45
   c. 167
   d. 27

34. How many ounces are in 2 cups?
   a. 4 oz.
   b. 8 oz.
   c. 16 oz.
   d. 10 oz.

35. The following temperatures were the highs during the second week of July.
   90°, 95°, 94°, 91°, 92°, 88°, 89°
   Arrange the temperatures from smallest to largest.
   a. 95°, 94°, 92°, 91°, 90°, 89°, 88°
   b. 90°, 91°, 88°, 89°, 92°, 94°, 95°
   c. 88°, 89°, 90°, 92°, 91°, 94°, 95°
   d. 88°, 89°, 90°, 91°, 92°, 94°, 95°

36. Which fraction of the circle is shaded? 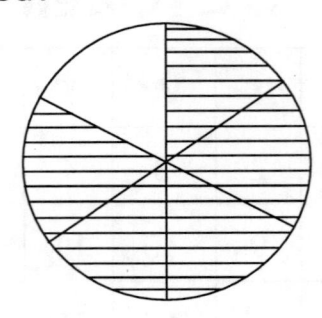
   a. $\frac{5}{6}$
   b. $\frac{1}{6}$
   c. $\frac{4}{7}$
   d. $\frac{7}{8}$

37. How many blocks were used to make this figure? 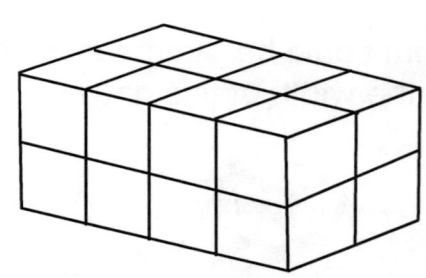
   a. 16
   b. 20
   c. 8
   d. 10

38. 16 =
   a. 8 × 3
   b. 4 × 4
   c. 4 × 3
   d. 16 × 0

39. What is the area?

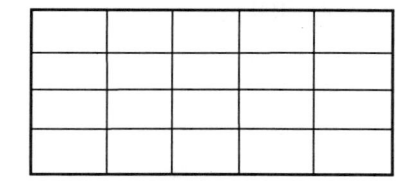

   a. 20
   b. 4
   c. 11
   d. 10

40. What is the sale price of a piano that regularly costs $5,000 and is $2,500 less than the regular price?
   a. $2,500
   b. $10,000
   c. $2,000
   d. $7,000

41. There are 10 desks in a row. How many rows will be needed for 50 students?
   a. 500 rows
   b. 5 rows
   c. 15 rows
   d. 50 rows

42. Solve.

   $$3\frac{6}{7} - 1\frac{1}{7} ?$$

   a. $4\frac{7}{7}$
   b. $2\frac{5}{0}$
   c. $2\frac{5}{7}$
   d. $3\frac{5}{7}$

43. ☐ × 8 = 64.
   a. 7
   b. 8
   c. 9
   d. 512

44. What is the area of the figure?

   10 [ ]
   5

   a. 50
   b. 15
   c. 25
   d. 35

45. Which temperature is the highest?

Monday	107°
Tuesday	100°
Wednesday	95°
Thursday	108°
Friday	99°

   a. 108°
   b. 107°
   c. 95°
   d. 100°

46. How many faces does this figure have?

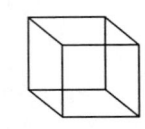

   a. 4
   b. 8
   c. 6
   d. 7

47. Which figure does not belong to this group?

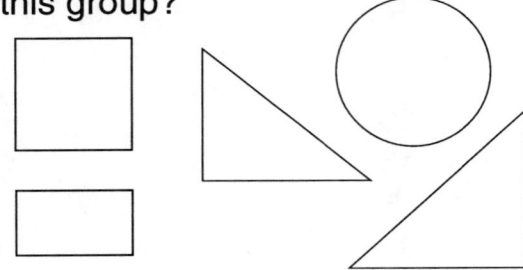

   a.
   b.
   c.
   d.

48. 2,000 + 100 + 4 = _____.
   a. 2,104
   b. 2,140
   c. 2,100
   d. 4,214

49. All of these are obtuse angles except_____.
   a.
   b.
   c.
   d.

50. What type of angle is ∠ABC?

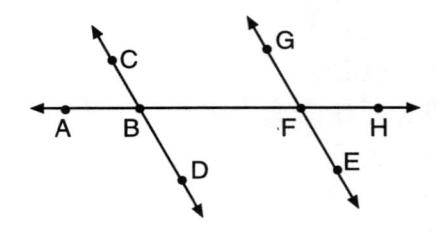

   a. line
   b. acute
   c. right
   d. obtuse

51. Which statement is not true?

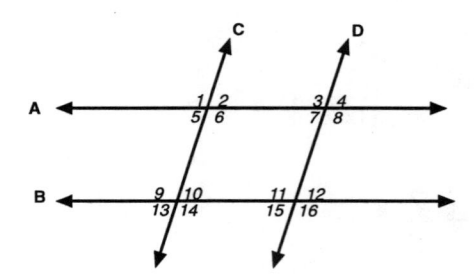

   a. Angles 2 and 10 are acute angles.
   b. Angles 1 and 3 are obtuse angles.
   c. Angles 10 and 12 are acute angles.
   d. Angles 2 and 4 are right angles.

Copyright © 1999 Contemporary Publishing Company of Raleigh, Inc.

52. The canoe trip took 2 and a half hours. How many minutes was this?
    a. 120
    b. 2.5
    c. 150
    d. 180

53. Which number falls between 136 and 147?
    a. 124
    b. 148
    c. 139
    d. 135

54. What is the perimeter of a triangle with sides of 15, 18, and 20?
    a. 43
    b. 63
    c. 70
    d. 53

55. What 3-dimensional figure would you make if you folded this 2-dimensional pattern?

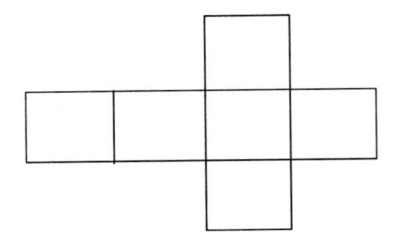

    a. triangle
    b. rectangle
    c. cube
    d. pyramid

56. Which figure is similar to the figure below?

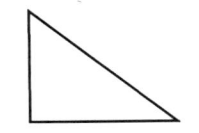

    a. 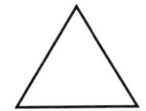
    b. 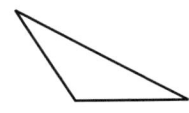
    c. 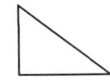
    d.

57. Which statement is true?

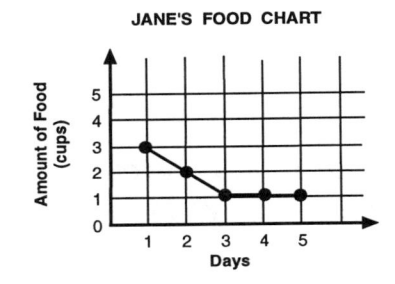

    JANE'S FOOD CHART

    a. The amount of food increased the first two days and decreased the last three.
    b. The amount of food eaten remained the same each day.
    c. The amount of food decreased, and then remained the same.
    d. The amount of food decreased the first two days and increased the last three.

58. $\square \div 2 = 10$
    a. 20
    b. 5
    c. 12
    d. 30

59. Which fractions are not equivalent?
   a. $\frac{2}{3} = \frac{4}{6}$
   b. $\frac{4}{9} = \frac{8}{18}$
   c. $\frac{1}{5} = \frac{3}{15}$
   d. $\frac{1}{2} = \frac{4}{10}$

60. Two pints of ice cream would equal _____.
   a. 1 quart
   b. 1 gallon
   c. 2 cups
   d. 3 ounces

61. Which team has twice as many women as men?

Teams	Men	Women
I	163	75
II	75	150
III	81	36
IV	103	91

   a. I
   b. II
   c. III
   d. IV

62. Which of these figures is 1/8 shaded?
   a. 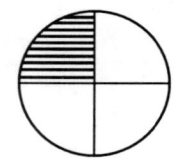
   b. 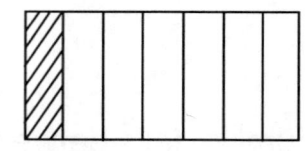
   c. 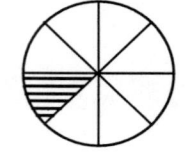
   d.

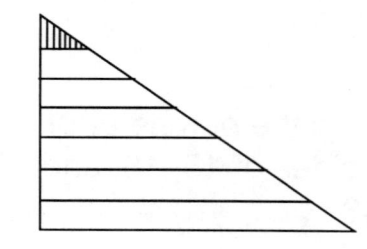

63. Which is true?
   a. 1 ounce = 16 pounds
   b. 1 ton = 3,000 pounds
   c. 1 pound = 16 ounces
   d. 36 inches = 1 foot

64. Which statement is true concerning this graph?

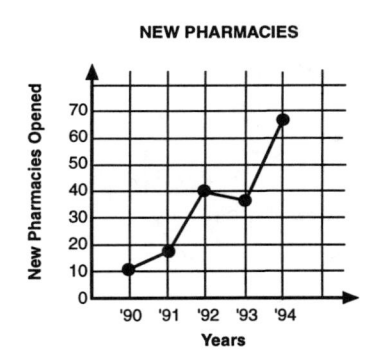

NEW PHARMACIES

a. The number of new pharmacies opened declined every year.
b. The number of pharmacies opened in 1992 equaled the number opened in 1993.
c. The largest number of new pharmacies opened during 1994.
d. 1990 and 1991 were the two years with the greatest number of new stores opened.

65. How much money is shown?

a. 67¢
b. 59¢
c. 45¢
d. 47¢

66. Marlowe was in Germany for 28 days. How many weeks is that?
a. 2
b. 12
c. 4
d. 3

67. What is another way to express 75 minutes?
a. 1 hour and 15 minutes
b. 2 hours and 5 minutes
c. 1 hour and 25 minutes
d. 3 hours

68. Which figure has only <u>one</u> line of symmetry?
a. 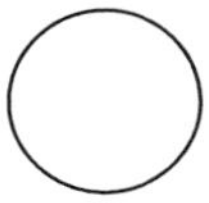   b. 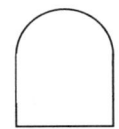
c.    d.

69. A new bicycle costs $199.95. What is the cost rounded to the nearest dollar?
a. $198
b. $201
c. $199
d. $200

70. What time will the clock read in 1 hour and 35 minutes?

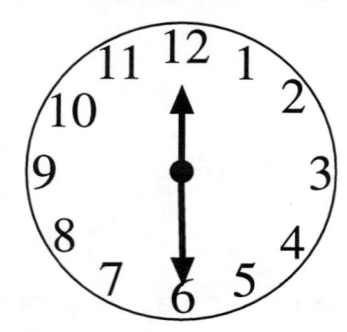

a. 2:00
b. 1:29
c. 1:35
d. 2:05

71. Mary Ruth must put ribbon around the edge of this napkin. How much ribbon will she need?

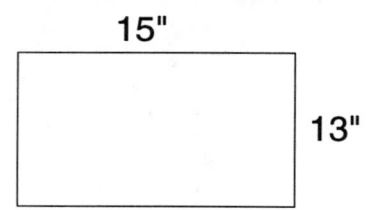

15"
13"

a. 28 inches
b. 30 inches
c. 56 inches
d. 195 inches

72. Which 3 colors of pencils total 50% of pencils bought?

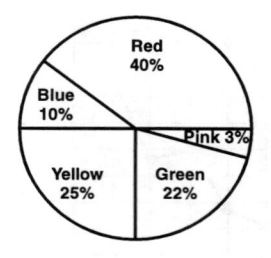

a. blue, red, pink
b. yellow, blue, green
c. red, green, pink
d. yellow, green, pink

73. How many dimes are in $5.00?
a. 5
b. 50
c. 15
d. 25

74. What kind of figure is this?

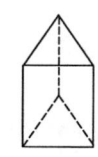

a. triangle
b. rectangular prism
c. triangular prism
d. pentagon

75. What time is it?

   3:15

   a. three forty-five
   b. three thirty
   c. quarter after three
   d. fifteen minutes before three

76. What is the difference in the area of a rectangle with 12,456 square feet and a triangle with 5,432 square feet?
   a. 129,992 sq. ft.
   b. 18,888 sq. ft.
   c. 17,888 sq. ft.
   d. 7,024 sq. ft.

77. What is the pattern?
   1, 3, 5, 7, 9
   a. +2
   b. −4
   c. ×2
   d. −1

78. [∴] [∴] [∴] [∴] =
   a. 4 ÷ 4 = 1
   b. 12 ÷ 3 = 4
   c. 15 ÷ 3 = 5
   d. 4 × 3 = 12

79. What is the closest estimate for this problem?
   36
   + 60
   a. 96
   b. 90
   c. 100
   d. 85

80. What is the highest exam grade?
   68, 75, 93, 67, 95, 50, 90, 67, 92, 91
   a. 67
   b. 68
   c. 95
   d. 93

Copyright © 1999 Contemporary Publishing Company of Raleigh, Inc.

Practice Test 2

Use answer sheet provided in the back of this book.

1. Arrange these temperatures from largest to smallest?
   92°, 75°, 87°, 36°, 41°, 80°, 91°
   a. 36°, 41°, 85°, 80°, 87°, 91°, 92°
   b. 92°, 91°, 87°, 75°, 80°, 41°, 36°
   c. 92°, 91°, 87°, 80°, 75°, 41°, 36°
   d. 36°, 41°, 75°, 87°, 80°, 91°, 92°

2. 3,125 + 295 + 40 =?
   a. 3,460
   b. 4,640
   c. 4,360
   d. 3,560

3. What is this figure?

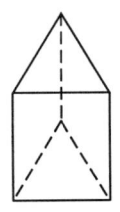

   a. octagon
   b. cone
   c. pentagon
   d. triangular prism

4. Which of the following is an example of translation?
   a.
   b.
   c.
   d.

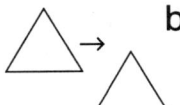

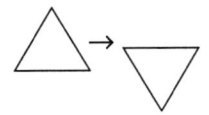

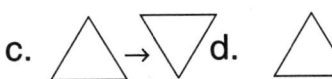

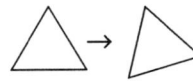

5. If one coconut cake costs $7.55, what is the best estimate for the cost of 8 cakes?
   a. $48
   b. $80
   c. $64
   d. $56

6. Lynn spends 5 hours of each 24 hour day sewing. How would you write this as a fractional part of her day?
   a. $\frac{5}{24}$
   b. $\frac{24}{5}$
   c. $\frac{19}{24}$
   d. $\frac{24}{19}$

7. Marlowe wants to write a 49 page book in one week. How many pages must she write each day?
   a. 10
   b. 3
   c. 7
   d. 6

8. $5\overline{)10}$ =
   a. 50
   b. 4
   c. 1
   d. 2

Copyright © 1999 Contemporary Publishing Company of Raleigh, Inc.

9. What would this figure look like if it shrank?

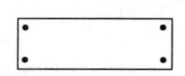

a. 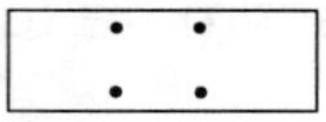 b. 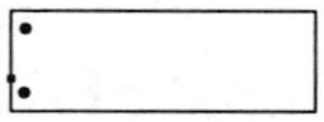 c.  d.

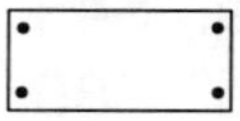

10. What shapes make up this figure?

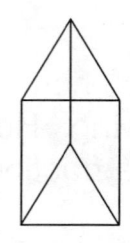

a. 4 rectangles and 2 pyramids
b. 2 triangles and 3 rectangles
c. 3 rectangles and 2 cubes
d. 2 triangles and 4 rectangles

11. Which is the same as (equivalent to) $\frac{1}{9}$?

a. $\frac{3}{4}$
b. $\frac{3}{6}$
c. $\frac{2}{18}$
d. $\frac{4}{20}$

12. $\square \times 6 = 36$?
a. 6
b. 4
c. 5
d. 9

13. What is the perimeter of this triangle?

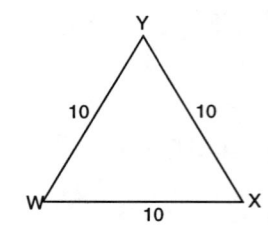

a. 300
b. 10
c. 30
d. 100

14. What is the bottom view of

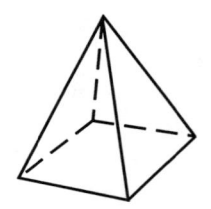

a. 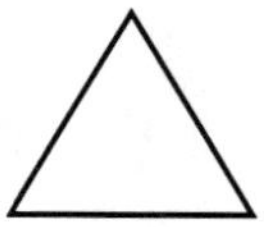 b. 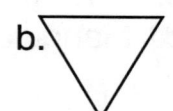 c. d.

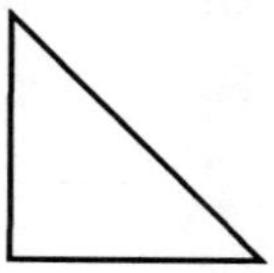

15. If John is walking 2 miles per hour, how long will it take him to walk 10 miles?
    a. 12 hours
    b. 20 hours
    c. 5 hours
    d. 8 hours

16. Name the ordered pair for the letter X on the grid.

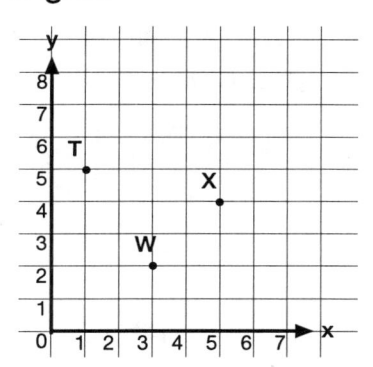

    a. (4, 4)
    b. (5, 4)
    c. (3, 3)
    d. (6, 4)

17. Using the pattern, what is the missing value of y?

x	y
2	4
1	3
0	?

    a. 1
    b. 2
    c. 4
    d. 0

18. Which statement is not true?

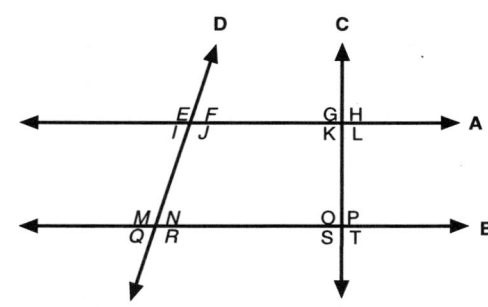

    a. ∠G and ∠H are right angles.
    b. ∠F and ∠N are acute angles.
    c. ∠M and ∠N are obtuse angles.
    d. ∠O and ∠T are right angles.

19. What number represents C?

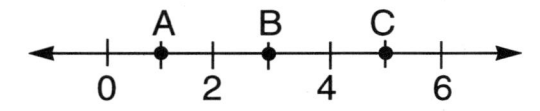

    a. 5
    b. 1
    c. 2
    d. 4

20. A tile floor is 15 ft. by 10 ft. How many feet of border will be needed to go around the floor?
    a. 25
    b. 100
    c. 35
    d. 50

21. What type of graph is shown?

Weekly Low Temperatures

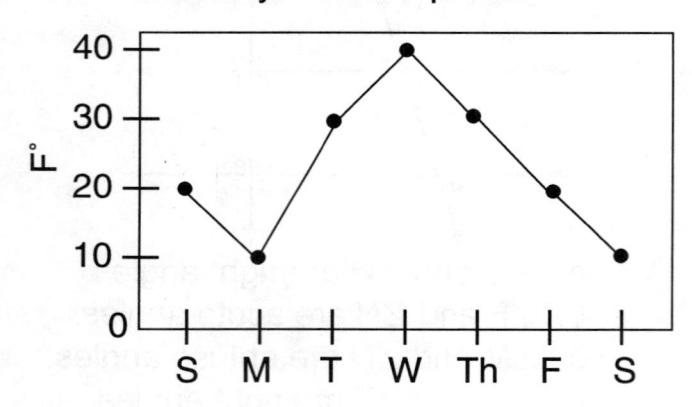

a. bar graph
b. circle graph
c. pictograph
d. line graph

22. What would be the next number in 0, 4, 8, 12, 16, ____ ?
a. 28
b. 24
c. +4
d. 20

23. If the input is 12, what is the output?

Input	Output
0	0
1	4
2	8
3	12

a. 16
b. 144
c. 36
d. 48

24. If this pattern continues, how many laps would be done in 6 hours?

HOURS	LAPS
1	30
2	60
3	120
4	240

a. 480
b. 2,160
c. 720
d. 960

25. What problem does the shaded part of this picture represent?

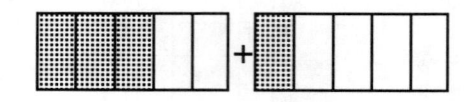

a. $\frac{2}{5} + \frac{4}{5} = \frac{6}{5}$
b. $\frac{3}{5} - \frac{1}{5} = \frac{2}{5}$
c. $\frac{3}{5} + \frac{1}{5} = \frac{4}{5}$
d. $\frac{3}{5} - \frac{3}{5} = 0$

26. Which color was liked best?

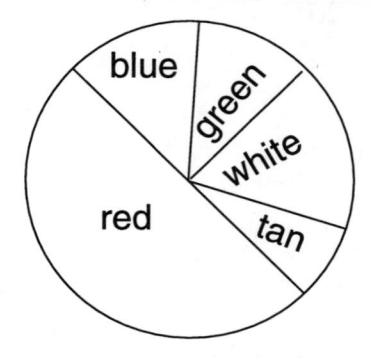

a. blue
b. tan
c. green
d. red

27. What is the 3-dimensional figure shown below?
    Side View   Bottom View

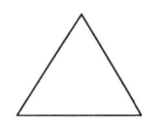

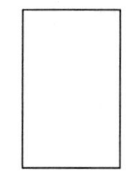

    a. cube
    b. rectangular prism
    c. triangular prism
    d. cylinder

28.

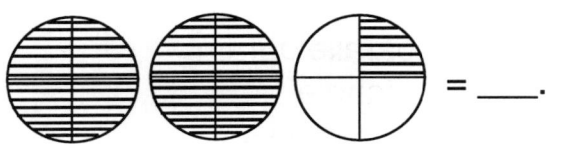

    a. $2\frac{1}{4}$
    b. $1\frac{1}{4}$
    c. $2\frac{3}{4}$
    d. $3\frac{1}{4}$

29. $30 \div 5$

    a. 4
    b. 25
    c. 7
    d. 6

30. Lynn scored 90, 80, 85, 95, 80, 70, and 100 on her science tests. What is the lowest score?
    a. 70
    b. 100
    c. 80
    d. 85

31. Put these temperatures in order from smallest to largest.
    25°, 45°, 50°, 125°, 15°, 21°
    a. 15°, 25°, 45°, 21°, 125°, 50°
    b. 50°, 25°, 21°, 45°, 125°, 15°
    c. 45°, 25°, 15°, 21°, 125°, 50°
    d. 15°, 21°, 25°, 45°, 50°, 125°

32. What is the best estimate for the solution of this problem?
    $55 + 71$
    a. 140
    b. 120
    c. 126
    d. 130

33. Margaret found 24 eggs at the Easter egg hunt. How many dozen eggs did she find?
    a. 1
    b. 3
    c. 4
    d. 2

34. What figure is shown on this graph?

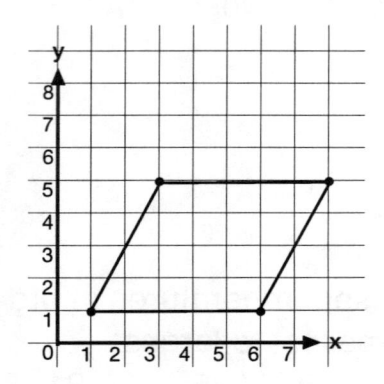

   a. square
   b. triangle
   c. parallelogram
   d. rectangle

35. How many feet are in 8 yards?
   a. 21
   b. 36
   c. 11
   d. 24

36. Marjorie bought a dress for $45.99. How much change did she receive from $50.00?
   a. $5.99
   b. $4.89
   c. $5.01
   d. $4.01

37. What shape is made when you graph these points in a coordinate plane and connect the points?
   (1, 1), (4, 1), (6, 3), (2, 3)

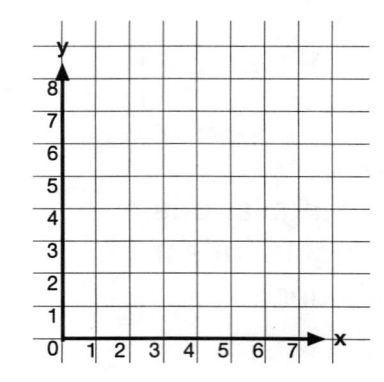

   a. parallelogram
   b. triangle
   c. rectangle
   d. square

38. Bud has 3 quarters and 2 dimes. How much money does he have?
   a. 40¢
   b. $1.00
   c. 85¢
   d. 95¢

39. $\square \div 2 = 7$
   a. 16
   b. 27
   c. 14
   d. 3

40. $3\frac{7}{8} - 1\frac{4}{8} =$
    a. $4\frac{11}{8}$
    b. $2\frac{3}{8}$
    c. $1\frac{3}{16}$
    d. $2\frac{3}{0}$

41. How many inches are in 3 feet?
    a. 120
    b. 22
    c. 36
    d. $3\frac{1}{3}$

42. $\frac{1}{4} + \frac{1}{4} =$
    a. $\frac{1}{8}$
    b. $\frac{1}{16}$
    c. $\frac{2}{4} = \frac{1}{2}$
    d. $\frac{2}{16} = \frac{1}{8}$

43. What is the area of this rectangle? (A = lw)
    a. 22
    b. 11
    c. 18
    d. 7

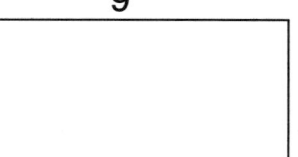

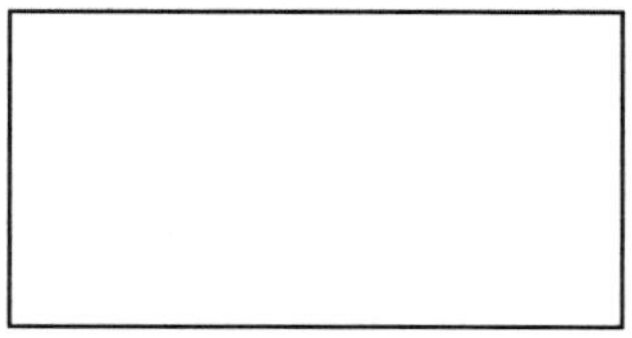

44. What is the name of this figure? 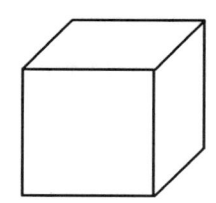
    a. cube
    b. rectangular prism
    c. rectangle
    d. rhombus

45. If May puts 5 apples in a basket every minute, and Connie takes out 1 apple from the basket every minute, how many apples are in the basket after 4 minutes? (The basket started empty!)
    a. 13
    b. 17
    c. 12
    d. 16

46. What is the total weight of Sal, Tom, and John?

NAME	AGE	WEIGHT
Callie	15	100
Sal	25	123
Tom	30	205
John	45	195

    a. 723
    b. 523
    c. 423
    d. 428

47. Juan has $10, and Araceli has $14. How many dimes do they have altogether? Which would be the best way to solve this problem?
   a. ($10 ÷ $14) × 10¢
   b. ($10 + $14) ÷ 10¢
   c. ($10 + $14) × 10¢
   d. 10¢ + $10 + $14

48. How many blocks are in this figure? 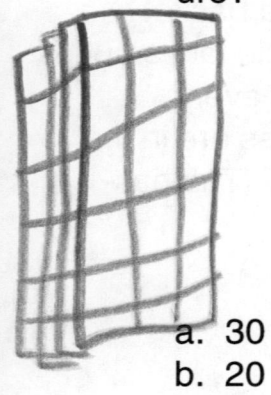 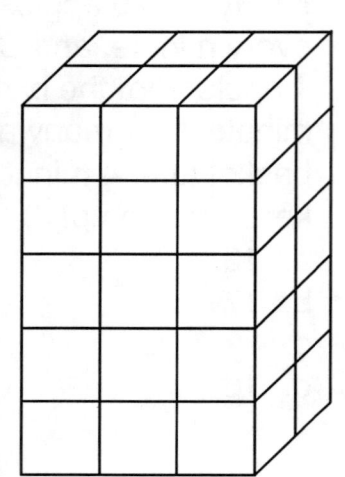
   a. 30
   b. 20
   c. 15
   d. 50

49. What is the temperature?
   a. 50°
   b. 40°
   c. 52°
   d. 62°

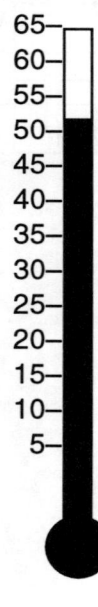

50. What triangle is similar to triangle C?
   a. D 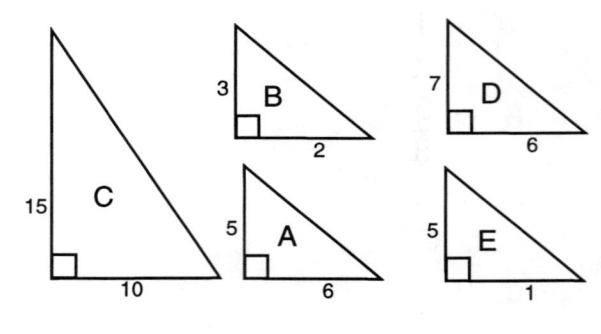
   b. E
   c. B
   d. A

51. All giraffes are tall. Kelsey is a giraffe. Which statement is true?
   a. Kelsey is not tall.
   b. Kelsey is tall.
   c. Kelsey is not a giraffe.
   d. Nothing can be determined.

52. At the circus, the audience ate 1,000 hotdogs. Each hotdog costs $1.99. Which of the following can be found from this information?
   a. How many people ate hotdogs?
   b. How much did the buns cost?
   c. How many hotdogs did Mr. Watts eat?
   d. How much money was spent on hotdogs?

53. Between what 2 consecutive years was there a decrease in sales?

CLASS RINGS BOUGHT

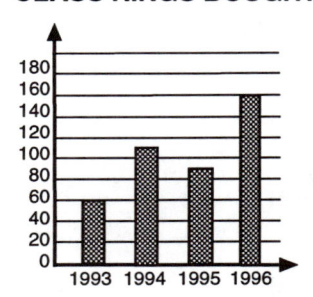

a. 1996 – 1993
b. 1995 – 1996
c. 1994 – 1995
d. 1995 – 1993

54. 1,350 – 286 = _____.
a. 1,136
b. 1,636
c. 1,076
d. 1,064

55. Graph (3, 11), (1, 5), (6, 5). What is the shape of this figure?

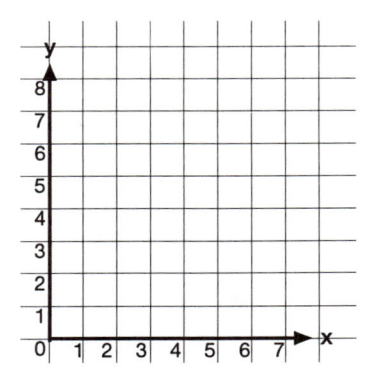

a. square
b. triangle
c. rectangle
d. circle

56. Margaret bought 7 cases of soda. Each case contains 10 cans of soda. How many cans of soda did she buy?
   Which sentence would you use to solve this problem?
a. 10 ÷ 7
b. 10 + 7
c. 10 × 7
d. 10 – 7

57. What type of angle is ∠a?

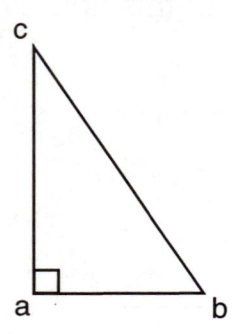

a. straight
b. acute
c. obtuse
d. right

58. How many feet are in 9 yards?
a. 27
b. 81
c. 108
d. 3

59. What time is it?

a. 4:30
b. 3:30
c. 4:00
d. 4:45

60. There are 4 seeds in each pot. If there are 9 pots, how many seeds are there?
a. 5
b. 13
c. 27
d. 36

61. Joyce walked 8 4/5 miles last Saturday. George walked 3 3/5 miles. How many more miles did Joyce walk?
a. $11 \frac{7}{5}$ mi.
b. $5 \frac{1}{5}$ mi.
c. $12 \frac{3}{5}$ mi.
d. $5 \frac{7}{5}$ mi.

62. Which fraction is equivalent (the same as) $\frac{8}{9}$?
a. $\frac{40}{54}$
b. $\frac{24}{36}$
c. $\frac{16}{27}$
d. $\frac{32}{36}$

63. Socks are on sale: 3 pairs for $10.00. The socks are regularly $4 per pair. How much would 6 pairs cost at the regular price?
a. $60
b. $4
c. $20
d. $24

64. Find the perimeter of this parallelogram.

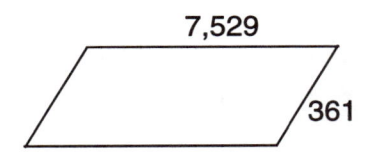

   7,529 / 361

   a. 22,278
   b. 2,717,969
   c. 11,139
   d. 13,589,845

65. What number is missing?

Input	Output
3	15
4	20
5	25
6	?

   a. 18
   b. 24
   c. 26
   d. 30

66. What is the name of this geometric solid?

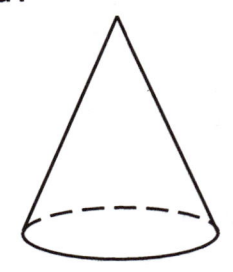

   a. pyramid
   b. cone
   c. triangular prism
   d. sphere

67. How much money is shown?

   a. 67¢
   b. 27¢
   c. 37¢
   d. 15¢

68. Which fractions are equivalent?
   a. $\frac{1}{2} = \frac{2}{3}$
   b. $\frac{3}{8} = \frac{6}{24}$
   c. $\frac{8}{12} = \frac{16}{24}$
   d. $\frac{4}{5} = \frac{20}{30}$

69. How much would you pay for 10 tickets?

   CONCERT TICKETS
   1st 4 tickets – $4.00 each
   Every ticket over 4 – $2.00 each

   a. $40
   b. $20
   c. $28
   d. $60

70. Round 127 to the nearest ten.
   a. 120
   b. 100
   c. 127
   d. 130

71. 2,176 = _____.
   a. 200 + 10 + 7 + 6
   b. 2,000 + 700 + 10 + 6
   c. 2,000 + 100 + 7 + 6
   d. 2,000 + 100 + 70 + 6

72. There are 12 green chips, 10 blue chips, 15 yellow chips, and 24 white chips in a bag. How many chips are in the bag?
   a. 51
   b. 70
   c. 60
   d. 61

73. Which unit is most appropriate to measure the width of an airplane?
   a. meter
   b. centimeter
   c. millimeter
   d. decimeter

74. Which model shows 1/2 of 1/3?
   a.   b.
   c.   d.

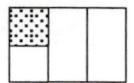

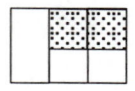

75. A city elementary school has an enrollment of 500 students. On a snow make up day, 250 of the students were absent. How many students attended school that day?
   a. 500
   b. 250
   c. 1,000
   d. 425

76. What is the next symbol in this sequence?
   ● ● ○ ○ ● ○ ● ● ○ ○ ● ○
   a. ● ● ●
   b. ●
   c. ○
   d. ○ ○

77. Which is the largest number?
   a. 8,000
   b. 8,003
   c. 7,999
   d. 8,002

78. What is the 5th month of every year?
   a. April
   b. July
   c. May
   d. March

79. Which of the following is not a line of symmetry?
   a. 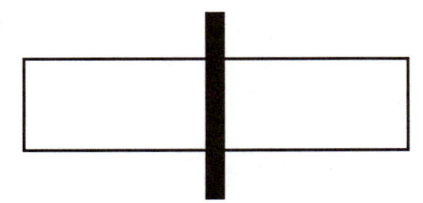
   b. 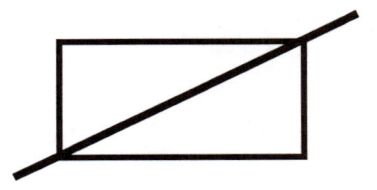
   c. 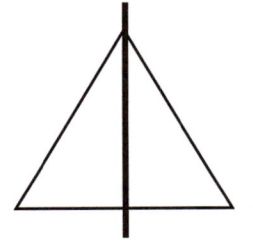
   d.

80. Cassie will have a scout meeting in 5 days. Today is Monday. What day is her meeting?
   a. Saturday
   b. Friday
   c. Sunday
   d. Thursday

ANSWER SHEET

EOG 3 MATHEMATICS PRACTICE TEST 1

Name_____

INSTRUCTIONS:
1. Fill in your name at the top of this page.
2. Tear out this page.
3. Solve each problem and fill in the appropriate bubbles (a, b, c, or d) on this sheet.

1. ⓐ ⓑ ⓒ ⓓ	21. ⓐ ⓑ ⓒ ⓓ	41. ⓐ ⓑ ⓒ ⓓ	61. ⓐ ⓑ ⓒ ⓓ
2. ⓐ ⓑ ⓒ ⓓ	22. ⓐ ⓑ ⓒ ⓓ	42. ⓐ ⓑ ⓒ ⓓ	62. ⓐ ⓑ ⓒ ⓓ
3. ⓐ ⓑ ⓒ ⓓ	23. ⓐ ⓑ ⓒ ⓓ	43. ⓐ ⓑ ⓒ ⓓ	63. ⓐ ⓑ ⓒ ⓓ
4. ⓐ ⓑ ⓒ ⓓ	24. ⓐ ⓑ ⓒ ⓓ	44. ⓐ ⓑ ⓒ ⓓ	64. ⓐ ⓑ ⓒ ⓓ
5. ⓐ ⓑ ⓒ ⓓ	25. ⓐ ⓑ ⓒ ⓓ	45. ⓐ ⓑ ⓒ ⓓ	65. ⓐ ⓑ ⓒ ⓓ
6. ⓐ ⓑ ⓒ ⓓ	26. ⓐ ⓑ ⓒ ⓓ	46. ⓐ ⓑ ⓒ ⓓ	66. ⓐ ⓑ ⓒ ⓓ
7. ⓐ ⓑ ⓒ ⓓ	27. ⓐ ⓑ ⓒ ⓓ	47. ⓐ ⓑ ⓒ ⓓ	67. ⓐ ⓑ ⓒ ⓓ
8. ⓐ ⓑ ⓒ ⓓ	28. ⓐ ⓑ ⓒ ⓓ	48. ⓐ ⓑ ⓒ ⓓ	68. ⓐ ⓑ ⓒ ⓓ
9. ⓐ ⓑ ⓒ ⓓ	29. ⓐ ⓑ ⓒ ⓓ	49. ⓐ ⓑ ⓒ ⓓ	69. ⓐ ⓑ ⓒ ⓓ
10. ⓐ ⓑ ⓒ ⓓ	30. ⓐ ⓑ ⓒ ⓓ	50. ⓐ ⓑ ⓒ ⓓ	70. ⓐ ⓑ ⓒ ⓓ
11. ⓐ ⓑ ⓒ ⓓ	31. ⓐ ⓑ ⓒ ⓓ	51. ⓐ ⓑ ⓒ ⓓ	71. ⓐ ⓑ ⓒ ⓓ
12. ⓐ ⓑ ⓒ ⓓ	32. ⓐ ⓑ ⓒ ⓓ	52. ⓐ ⓑ ⓒ ⓓ	72. ⓐ ⓑ ⓒ ⓓ
13. ⓐ ⓑ ⓒ ⓓ	33. ⓐ ⓑ ⓒ ⓓ	53. ⓐ ⓑ ⓒ ⓓ	73. ⓐ ⓑ ⓒ ⓓ
14. ⓐ ⓑ ⓒ ⓓ	34. ⓐ ⓑ ⓒ ⓓ	54. ⓐ ⓑ ⓒ ⓓ	74. ⓐ ⓑ ⓒ ⓓ
15. ⓐ ⓑ ⓒ ⓓ	35. ⓐ ⓑ ⓒ ⓓ	55. ⓐ ⓑ ⓒ ⓓ	75. ⓐ ⓑ ⓒ ⓓ
16. ⓐ ⓑ ⓒ ⓓ	36. ⓐ ⓑ ⓒ ⓓ	56. ⓐ ⓑ ⓒ ⓓ	76. ⓐ ⓑ ⓒ ⓓ
17. ⓐ ⓑ ⓒ ⓓ	37. ⓐ ⓑ ⓒ ⓓ	57. ⓐ ⓑ ⓒ ⓓ	77. ⓐ ⓑ ⓒ ⓓ
18. ⓐ ⓑ ⓒ ⓓ	38. ⓐ ⓑ ⓒ ⓓ	58. ⓐ ⓑ ⓒ ⓓ	78. ⓐ ⓑ ⓒ ⓓ
19. ⓐ ⓑ ⓒ ⓓ	39. ⓐ ⓑ ⓒ ⓓ	59. ⓐ ⓑ ⓒ ⓓ	79. ⓐ ⓑ ⓒ ⓓ
20. ⓐ ⓑ ⓒ ⓓ	40. ⓐ ⓑ ⓒ ⓓ	60. ⓐ ⓑ ⓒ ⓓ	80. ⓐ ⓑ ⓒ ⓓ

ANSWER SHEET

EOG 3 MATHEMATICS PRACTICE TEST 2

Name_____

INSTRUCTIONS:

1. Fill in your name at the top of this page.
2. Tear out this page.
3. Solve each problem and fill in the appropriate bubbles (a, b, c, or d) on this sheet.

1. ⓐ ⓑ ⓒ ⓓ	21. ⓐ ⓑ ⓒ ⓓ	41. ⓐ ⓑ ⓒ ⓓ	61. ⓐ ⓑ ⓒ ⓓ
2. ⓐ ⓑ ⓒ ⓓ	22. ⓐ ⓑ ⓒ ⓓ	42. ⓐ ⓑ ⓒ ⓓ	62. ⓐ ⓑ ⓒ ⓓ
3. ⓐ ⓑ ⓒ ⓓ	23. ⓐ ⓑ ⓒ ⓓ	43. ⓐ ⓑ ⓒ ⓓ	63. ⓐ ⓑ ⓒ ⓓ
4. ⓐ ⓑ ⓒ ⓓ	24. ⓐ ⓑ ⓒ ⓓ	44. ⓐ ⓑ ⓒ ⓓ	64. ⓐ ⓑ ⓒ ⓓ
5. ⓐ ⓑ ⓒ ⓓ	25. ⓐ ⓑ ⓒ ⓓ	45. ⓐ ⓑ ⓒ ⓓ	65. ⓐ ⓑ ⓒ ⓓ
6. ⓐ ⓑ ⓒ ⓓ	26. ⓐ ⓑ ⓒ ⓓ	46. ⓐ ⓑ ⓒ ⓓ	66. ⓐ ⓑ ⓒ ⓓ
7. ⓐ ⓑ ⓒ ⓓ	27. ⓐ ⓑ ⓒ ⓓ	47. ⓐ ⓑ ⓒ ⓓ	67. ⓐ ⓑ ⓒ ⓓ
8. ⓐ ⓑ ⓒ ⓓ	28. ⓐ ⓑ ⓒ ⓓ	48. ⓐ ⓑ ⓒ ⓓ	68. ⓐ ⓑ ⓒ ⓓ
9. ⓐ ⓑ ⓒ ⓓ	29. ⓐ ⓑ ⓒ ⓓ	49. ⓐ ⓑ ⓒ ⓓ	69. ⓐ ⓑ ⓒ ⓓ
10. ⓐ ⓑ ⓒ ⓓ	30. ⓐ ⓑ ⓒ ⓓ	50. ⓐ ⓑ ⓒ ⓓ	70. ⓐ ⓑ ⓒ ⓓ
11. ⓐ ⓑ ⓒ ⓓ	31. ⓐ ⓑ ⓒ ⓓ	51. ⓐ ⓑ ⓒ ⓓ	71. ⓐ ⓑ ⓒ ⓓ
12. ⓐ ⓑ ⓒ ⓓ	32. ⓐ ⓑ ⓒ ⓓ	52. ⓐ ⓑ ⓒ ⓓ	72. ⓐ ⓑ ⓒ ⓓ
13. ⓐ ⓑ ⓒ ⓓ	33. ⓐ ⓑ ⓒ ⓓ	53. ⓐ ⓑ ⓒ ⓓ	73. ⓐ ⓑ ⓒ ⓓ
14. ⓐ ⓑ ⓒ ⓓ	34. ⓐ ⓑ ⓒ ⓓ	54. ⓐ ⓑ ⓒ ⓓ	74. ⓐ ⓑ ⓒ ⓓ
15. ⓐ ⓑ ⓒ ⓓ	35. ⓐ ⓑ ⓒ ⓓ	55. ⓐ ⓑ ⓒ ⓓ	75. ⓐ ⓑ ⓒ ⓓ
16. ⓐ ⓑ ⓒ ⓓ	36. ⓐ ⓑ ⓒ ⓓ	56. ⓐ ⓑ ⓒ ⓓ	76. ⓐ ⓑ ⓒ ⓓ
17. ⓐ ⓑ ⓒ ⓓ	37. ⓐ ⓑ ⓒ ⓓ	57. ⓐ ⓑ ⓒ ⓓ	77. ⓐ ⓑ ⓒ ⓓ
18. ⓐ ⓑ ⓒ ⓓ	38. ⓐ ⓑ ⓒ ⓓ	58. ⓐ ⓑ ⓒ ⓓ	78. ⓐ ⓑ ⓒ ⓓ
19. ⓐ ⓑ ⓒ ⓓ	39. ⓐ ⓑ ⓒ ⓓ	59. ⓐ ⓑ ⓒ ⓓ	79. ⓐ ⓑ ⓒ ⓓ
20. ⓐ ⓑ ⓒ ⓓ	40. ⓐ ⓑ ⓒ ⓓ	60. ⓐ ⓑ ⓒ ⓓ	80. ⓐ ⓑ ⓒ ⓓ